THE
MAGIC
FIRE

BY LILLIAN GROAG

★

★

DRAMATISTS
PLAY SERVICE
INC.

THE MAGIC FIRE
Copyright © 2005, Lillian Groag

All Rights Reserved

SPECIAL NOTE

SPECIAL NOTE ON SONGS AND RECORDINGS

PRODUCTION NOTES

SET: The Bergs' apartment should have the necessary furniture, but perhaps no walls, although doors and windows are important. The impression should be of an old Paris, or West Side Manhattan apartment (around 104th – 106th St. and Riverside). In the background one might see the silhouettes of the various transatlantic liners typical of the Buenos Aires harbor at the time. Perhaps the basic set should include "abstracts" of Buenos Aires all around, the ubiquitous bistros, the corner street lamps, etc.

PERFORMANCE: It's a drama INSIDE a big comedy. The drama will take care of itself. The comedy will need attention to detail and a solid structure to support the seeming formlessness of the whole. All the important information is tucked away under the chatter. Points should be made sharply and quickly. The pace is very fast and light of touch. The intensity of discomfort and tension should grow in direct proportion to the amount of persiflage; i.e., these people are in most trouble when they least appear to be.

Act Two will need extensive verbal (as well as physical) choreography. Its apparent chaos was carefully constructed to let the undercurrent start and grow as the act moves along. If it's left to play wildly on its own, it turns to mud and no points are made. The overlaps have to be worked out so that the "A-line" conversation is heard by the audience while the "B-line" conversation under it is NOT pitched down in any way. It's as much a staging problem as a vocal one. When they sing "Il Balen," it's Dionysiac. They don't care that they are not opera singers, they let fly with the same passion and love of the music as the women in *Dancing at Lughnasa*. It's the crest of the act. Everything goes downhill from there.

ABOVE ANYTHING ELSE: These people are not "eccentrics," lovable or not, and they are not intellectuals. They just happen to go to the opera and like to read books. The only character who can be called "eccentric," but who is actually and tragically slowly letting go of reality, is Paula. She crashes in the epilogue scene at the docks, which should be a tragicomic scene. Not a single one of them is sentimental or in any way "cute," and the child is most definitely not "adorable" *nor precocious.* Her questions are simple, direct and honest and, if examined, appropriate for a seven-year-old.

3

LISE — the adult narrator — will weave in and out of the action. Several characters interact with her at times and then go on ignoring her.

MUSIC is a character in the play. The pieces called for as well as the actual musical phrases used are not optional. It should weave in and out of dialogue as part of it and take over when indicated, supported by scenic effects as complex or simple as deemed necessary by the director. For example, to underline the intensity of the girl's imaginary life — she can't play outside — the "Magic Fire" moment in Act One, Scene 1, just before Amalia's first entrance, could include a virtual transformation of the playing space into the Valkyrie's Rock complete with the shadow of Wotan crossing the fire, or simply a "fire" effect on the walls of the room which would intensify and drop with the music.

THE MAGIC FIRE was commissioned and originally produced by the Oregon Shakespeare Festival (Libby Appel, Artistic Director; Paul E. Nicholson, Executive Director) in Ashland, Oregon, opening on August 2, 1997. It was directed by Libby Appel; the set design was by Richard L. Hay; the costume design was by Deborah M. Dryden; the lighting design was by Ann G. Wrightson; the sound design was by Sara Jane Schmeltzer; the original music was by Todd Barton; the voice and text direction were by Nancy Benjamin; the movement direction was by John Sipes; the original choreography was by Xedex; the dramaturg was Lue Morgan Douthit; the stage manager was Susan L. McMillan; and the production assistant was Mark Mezadourian Hughes. The cast was as follows:

LISE .... Vilma Silva
YOUNG LISE .... Alyn McKenna Bartell
OTTO BERG .... Anthony Heald
AMALIA BERG .... Demetra Pittman
ELENA GUARNERI .... Judith-Marie Bergan
GIANNI "JUAN" GUARNERI .... Ken Albers
PAULA GUARNERI .... Dee Maaske
HENRI FONTANNES .... Richard Howard
ALBERTO BARCOS .... Michael J. Hume
MADDALENA GUARNERI .... Eileen DeSandre
ROSA ARRUA .... Robynn Rodriguez
CLARA STEPANECK .... Catherine E. Coulson
GIOVANNI GUARNERI .... Ken Albers
BLASINA GUARNERI .... Judith-Marie Bergan
YOUNG GIANNI "JUAN" .... Dylan Heald

THE MAGIC FIRE was developed by The Kennedy Center Fund for New American Plays and presented at The Kennedy Center in Washington, D.C., opening on November 7, 1998. It was directed by Libby Appel; the set design was by Richard L. Hay; the costume design was by Deborah M. Dryden; the lighting design was by Ann G. Wrightson; the sound design was by Sara Jane Schmeltzer; the original music was by Todd Barton; the voice and text direction were by Nancy Benjamin; the movement direction was by John Sipes; the original choreography was by Xedex; additional choreography was by David Hochoy; the dramaturg was Lue Morgan Douthit; and the stage manager was Susan L. McMillan. The cast was as follows:

LISE .... Vilma Silva
YOUNG LISE .... Alyn McKenna Bartell/Antonia Whitmore
OTTO BERG .... Anthony Heald
AMALIA BERG .... Demetra Pittman
ELENA GUARNERI .... Judith-Marie Bergan
GIANNI "JUAN" GUARNERI .... Ken Albers
PAULA GUARNERI .... Dee Maaske
HENRI FONTANNES .... Richard Howard
ALBERTO BARCOS .... Michael J. Hume
MADDALENA GUARNERI .... Eileen DeSandre
ROSA ARRUA .... Robynn Rodriguez
CLARA STEPANECK .... Catherine E. Coulson
GIOVANNI GUARNERI .... Ken Albers
BLASINA GUARNERI .... Judith-Marie Bergan
YOUNG GIANNI "JUAN" .... Dylan Heald

CHARACTERS

LISE as adult. Ironic, wry. A restless woman. She smokes.

LISE 2 — 7 years old. An unpleasant little girl. Two front teeth missing. Loud. In a state of permanent indignation. NEVER CUTE.

OTTO BERG (Lise's father) — 40s. Light Viennese accent. A quiet, gentle man. Glasses.

AMALIA BERG (his wife) — 35–40s. A beautiful, charming, rather vague woman. The steel hand under the kid glove. She controls the seemingly chaotic dinner party of Act Two.

ELENA GUARNERI (Amalia's sister) — 40s. Stunning, chic, Wry, witty, a stage star.

GIANNI "JUAN" GUARNERI (Amalia's father) — 70s. Light Italian accent. Big man, jovial, full of a watchful bonhomie.

PAULA GUARNERI (Juan's sister) — 60s. Delicate of frame, slightly wild-eyed, all flying scarves and wisps of hair. A somewhat startled shipwreck of the 1910s.

GENERAL HENRI FONTANNES (the Bergs' neighbor) —40s. Handsome, charismatic, charming, troubled.

ALBERTO BARCOS (A friend of the family) — 40s. An intellectual. He runs a newspaper.

MADDALENA GUARNERI (Juan's mother) — 98. Heavy Italian accent, hard of hearing, angry. Dragon Lady. NEVER CUTE.

ROSA ARRUA (The Bergs' housekeeper) — 40–50. Strong.

CLARA STEPANECK (Otto's aunt) — 60s. Viennese accent. Très ancien régime. Careful, watchful, elegant.

The following actors will play these roles at the dock in the Prologue:

GIOVANNI — by the actor playing his son Juan.

LEILA — by the actress playing Elena, or if the "ghost" is seen in Act Three, Scene 1, by some other innocent bystander.

PLACE

Buenos Aires.

TIME

June – July 1952.

"I come from a sad country."

—Jorge Luis Borges

"Remember music and beware."

—Anne Sexton
"The Wonderful Musician"

"We have to accept, however reluctantly, the simple fact that we live in an age of refugees, of migrants, vagrants, nomads roaming about the continents and warming their souls with the memory of their — spiritual or ethnic, divine or geographical, real or imaginary — homes. A total homelessness is unbearable; it would amount to a complete break with human existence. Is perfect cosmopolitanism possible? Diogenes Laertius reports that Anaxagoras, when asked if he did not care much about his motherland, replied that he did care very much indeed and pointed at the sky. Some people today make similar claims, denying any partial interest in, or special loyalty to, their original tribal community; to what extent this claim may be made in good faith is debatable."

—Leszek Kolakowski
The Times Literary Supplement
October 11, 1985

" ... the vicissitudes of time and politics erode the human urges to be virtuous and heroic."

—Ben Brantley
The New York Times
August 18, 1995

"Having sampled two oceans as well as continents, I feel that I know what the globe itself must feel: there's nowhere to go. Elsewhere is nothing more than a far-flung strew of stars, burning away."

—Joseph Brodsky

"We know that in his work Proust did not describe a life as it actually was, but a life as it was remembered by the one who had lived it."

—Walter Benjamin
Illuminations

"The best lack all conviction, while the worst are full of passionate intensity."

—Yeats

THE MAGIC FIRE

PROLOGUE

September 2001. In the dark, the first strains of a tango: "Mi Buenos Aires Querido," played on a single bandoneon. A pin spot on Lise.

LISE. I'm an immigrant in a country of immigrants. My family were immigrants in a country of immigrants. Vagabond times. Home, private and politic, is shifting ground under our feet with the heart looking forever back towards a vanishing point. And inevitably, halfway, "in the middle of the road," as they say, it suddenly becomes imperative to remember and we fumble in the dark for that switch that could make all the difference: But the source of light is long gone. *(She nervously fumbles for a cigarette. Lights it.)* I am an American now. Argentina drifts in and out of shadows through my mind like the ghost ship of *The Flying Dutchman*. The only certainty is the sudden bump inside the chest recalling with cutting clarity my mother's great beauty and my father's all-consuming passion for music. And that's no longer memory but a movement of the heart warming to the glow of what we first loved. Paradise lost. A flash: Coming home from school — first grade — on wet winter afternoons to the comforting hiss of the wall radiators that never quite kept the house warm and a bowl of steaming *caffé latte* and bread and butter in the kitchen, where Rosa listened to her radio soaps. *(Lights slowly up. A dishevelled, scowling little girl in blue convent uniform.)*

ROSA. Look at you! What've you been doing? What happened to your school uniform? Where's your hat? Have you been fighting again?

LISE 2. Marco Dormanowicz tried to kill me.

11

ROSA. He's seven years old!

LISE 2. He was lying in wait.

ROSA. He lives in the other direction!

LISE 2. *(Beat.)* Sometimes I take the long way home.

ROSA. And look at your pencil box. You broke it again!

LISE 2. Marco Dormanowicz ran into it.

LISE. Four times.

ROSA. Never seen such a nasty child.

LISE.	LISE 2.
Yeah.	Snot-nose creep.

ROSA. It's *you* I'm talking about, miss! *(Exiting with Lise 2.)* Let's go eat. See if I can sew those buttons back. Will you look at this mess!

LISE. I must have been in love with Marco Dormanowicz and thought it bewitching of me to walk past his doorstep where he invariably — and as it turned out, stupidly — sat, and bonk him over the head with my pencil box. I wish I could say that was the worst of it.

LISE 2. *(Quietly, on the telephone, feigned voice.)* Hello? Is this Marco Dormanowicz? This is the pound. We have your dog. We had to put him to sleep. *(She hangs up.)*

LISE. Patterns are set early in one's relationship to the opposite sex. Sounds: the discreet clanking of the wrought-iron elevator — was it black? — taking the preternaturally silent tenants of the apartment house into thickly carpeted halls. Muffled steps, quiet voices, closing doors and a sharp sense of something prowling past our windows which my parents were not eager to discuss. Above all: the silence. It had a name and a face. But she wasn't "Evita" in our house. She was "Eva Perón," or more often, "That Woman," and nobody I knew was going to be crying for *her.* All that winter black clouds clashed around the stone-grey Buenos Aires skyline as the city was presented with the macabre — and politically useful — spectacle of her slow public death. *(Music — prelude to* La Traviata.*)* Somehow I mixed it all up with the end of *Traviata* — which we seemed to be permanently listening to — there was a thrilling new Greek girl singing it now — so that last winter in Buenos Aires is scored in my mind with Verdi's music and the terrifying image of a beautiful young woman dying in a big house. *(The long, deep horn of a transatlantic steamer.)* Most Argentines we knew were children and grandchildren of immigrants. Some had come full of push and daring, like my great-grandfather Giovanni, in 1890. *(The ship's horn again. In the background, the dark outline* *of a transatlantic steamer appears against the sky. The docks. 1890. Italian accents.)*

GIOVANNI. *(Loaded with old, bursting suitcases.)* I raise the best horses, the best vineyards in America!

LISE. Whereas his wife was brought kicking and screaming all the way.

MADDALENA. Three weeks in *steerage* with smelly foreigners from Napoli!

GIOVANNI. New country! New world!

MADDALENA. What was wrong with the old one?

GIOVANNI. No land, no house, no cow.

MADDALENA. So?

GIOVANNI. Also no money, lousy government and scary neighbors.

MADDALENA. You want *everyting!*

GIOVANNI. We make new life. Good life. You see.

MADDALENA. *Then* we go home?

LISE. Other women, like my great-aunt Leila, came off the steamers blooming with youth and hope. She was eighteen. And the twenties were beginning to flap. *(The docks. Giovanni and Maddalena are there.)*

LEILA. *(Italian accent.)* So many stars! The Southern Cross! Where is Federico?

MADDALENA. You tell her.

GIOVANNI. He — married.

LEILA. *(Beat.)* He ... not wait...?

MADDALENA. The bitch is Corsican and she squints. He's a dead man.

GIOVANNI. Don't worry, *tesoro,* we find you better bridegroom with strong arms to hold forever, yes?

LEILA. *(Beat.)* Yes.

LISE. They never did find Leila the bridegroom with the strong arms "to hold forever" or even for a little while, and a chronic distrust of men bred a line of mule-headed spinsters with a deceivingly absent manner who outraged the rest of the family, all steadfastly, if often lugubriously, married.

GIOVANNI. What's the matter with you girls? You allergic to whiskers? If I didn't know better I would think you were — well, you know — *peculiar.*

LISE. But the "girls," too spirited not to rebel and too much of their time and place to know how, remained poised mid-gesture in perplexed loneliness, and considered eccentric past discretion, eventually became it. That's how my great-aunt Paula came to be called the March Hare and never knew it. We think.

PAULA. Oh, men are all right for special occasions, dear, but not for every day. They're not at their best indoors. They knock into the furniture and they're *very* hard on the china.

LISE. Finally, in 1938, there was the wave of refugees from the most recent European debacle that brought my father. *(The docks. 1938.)*

OTTO. *(Suitcase in one hand, a small Olivetti in the other. He's talking to someone we don't see.)* Here I am. No other luggage. Mostly my piano scores. Only the ones with the autographs. Couldn't leave those. *(Beat.)* I left in the middle of the night. *(Beat.)* This place now … it's — it looks — so — big. So … open. And the buildings, so … square! Everything … so … *(Dismayed.)* new…! Well, it's the New World! Are there decent coffeehouses? The Argentine Consul in Vienna gave me the name of a Chamber Music Society. How much money does the government give to the opera? Max and Edie? We haven't seen them for — some time. This can't possibly last. We're — *Viennese.* We're not — *like that …*

LISE. Papi wasn't just born in Vienna: he was born in the goddamn *Vienna Woods. (Music — Strauss'* Tales from the Vienna Woods. *The zither intro.)* He *walked* in three-quarter time. The Strauss waltz was his *only* national anthem. It went with him everywhere, through the rain-swept, policed streets, to the shabby, ill-lit office where he worked into the night. He took great pains to make sure we didn't confuse it with any other waltz.

OTTO. *(To Lise 2.)* You see, in an ordinary waltz the downbeat is just a *thud*; in the Viennese waltz the downbeat is "regret." *(Upstage in isolated light, Otto teaches Lise 2 how to waltz.* Tales of the Vienna Woods *now in full swing. They count omitting the "one.")*

LISE. And I acquired a residue of unearned ruefulness and by a sort of sentimental proxy, the weight of a past in which I had had no real part. What does one do with borrowed memory? It wasn't just Papi, of course. There were *two* modes of nostalgia in the house. The Viennese sort: *(Sound: Richard Tauber singing "Leise, ganz leise" from* Watzertraum: *"Leise, ganz leise, klingt's durch den Raum … " Clara and Otto sigh ruefully and elegantly.)* And the Italian sort: *(Sound: Franco Corelli howling "Cuore 'ngrato": "Cuooooooore, cuoooooooore 'ngraaato!" Amalia and the Italians sob violently and loudly.)* And nothing in between. Sunday afternoons, the opera broadcast. *(Everybody gathers around an old Zenith radio. Music —* La Bohème, *end of Act One duet. Immediate explosion.)*

ALL. *(Ad-lib. Shouting.)* The bum, he took it down! / That's what Puccini wrote! / See? Right here! Right here! / Give me that score! / Bullshit what Puccini wrote! Any tenor with *coglioni* — any tenor who calls himself *Italian* goes for a high C whenever he can! / Well this one's Russian! / Bulgarian! / What, they have no high C's in Bulgaria? / That's not a tenor, that's a *castrato!* / Well, she was off too! / She was not! / Please, the woman hasn't sung in an original key since World War I! / *Bolshevikkies* singing Puccini! / Caruso always took it up!

LISE. And the sun would stream through the windows and spill on the old red carpet as they carried on until Mimi died and then they wept —

LISE and LISE 2. — every time — !

LISE. — even my father, who, a snob about what called "the horrors of *verismo,*" kept a soft spot in his heart for *La Bohème* which to him sang the loss of that which is private and fragile and may count for nothing in the large scope of things. Something to do with ... with ...

OTTO. ... the fall of the sparrow ...

LISE. Everybody took it for granted that this "trip to America" was only "for a little while" and that once fortunes were made and balance restored in Europe, they were all going to go "back home." Nobody ever did, but they kept up the pretense anyway, growing old beside musty, moth-ridden steamer trunks with lost keys to rusty locks. An old *"Nonna,"* a *"Zia,"* a *"Tante,"* a *"Babushka"* in the spare room, that's the Argentina I remember; four different accents in one house and a tango crooning down a narrow hallway in a haze of Gauloise. Nonna Maddalena never saw her beloved Piemonte again, but resignation not being a family trait, she called her husband "The Welcher" to the end of her days and spent the war years going to movie theatres and jumping to her feet whenever Mussolini's Black Shirts goose-stepped through a newsreel, waving her cane in the dark, shouting in the midst of a terrified audience:

MADDALENA. *Fascisti maledetti! Mascalzoni! Vergogna! Vergogna! (The women drag her away, apologizing to imaginary people.)*

AD-LIBS. She's having one of her spells! / She's ninety-one / It's a fixation. / Time for Nonna's nap!

LISE. Never dreaming of a world where a classical education would prove as desirable as a pair of shorts in the Arctic Circle, my poor naive parents went about making sure that whatever else they lacked, their children would be educated.

15

OTTO. An education is all we can give you.

AMALIA. *(To Otto.)* We must be careful, darling. Men who go to great lengths to improve their intellect despise women who do the same. They much prefer them unencumbered of mind and full of body. They invariably marry pillows.

LISE. Their fondest belief that they were preparing me for "Life" catastrophically omitted to consider on what planet, their idea of pop being Tchaikovsky. *(Maddalena comes tearing out of the dark. The other women join her as they speak.)*

MADDALENA. I can see where she's going! It all gonna be *our fault!*

AMALIA. We did our best.

LISE. You sent me out there *unprepared!*

ELENA. You think everybody else gets a rehearsal?

CLARA. All childhoods are traumatic, even in the *best* of times.

AMALIA. Which these were not ...

LISE. What were you *thinking?!* People were dancing to the Stones while I tried to convince boys that *Liebestod* was sexy! My idea of a light flirtation was straight out of the Brontës! I made Proust jokes at parties! *In French! (Alarmed clucking from the women.)* It was *gruesome!*

AMALIA. Too much music. I kept telling him.

ROSA. Too many cuckoos. Not enough fresh air.

PAULA. What does she mean, "cuckoos"?

AMALIA. We did our best!

LISE. I just want to — to know —

MADDALENA. What? What you wanna know? Nobody know nothin'. Ever.

LISE. What makes me such a stranger ... everywhere ...

MADDALENA. You *tink* you turn us into theatre, we go away? We *never* go away. *(To the others.)* See now she's gonna make us do things we did not do, say things we did not say. Worse, she gonna guess what we *meant! (Great alarm from everybody. To Lise.)* What do you know? You wasn't there in the beginning! *(To audience.)* Get your money back. Go home. She don't know. I leave from *Genova,* two in the morning. NOBODY ASK ME! I WAS KIDNAPPÈD! I have two small children. We go through Gibraltar, and I never see my blue *Mediterraneo* again. I look back, I see rock, I look ahead, I see grey, I look sideways, I see people throwing up ... been that way ever since ... *(She is dragged off by the others with a great to-do.)*

AD LIBS. Who let her out? / She got away from me! / She climbs down windows, I've seen her! / One day the police is going to take

16

you away, Nonna! / NONNA. *Carabinieri! Fascisti!* Sonsa-bitches, shoot 'em all! / *(The women.)* A little linden tea? / *(Paula.)* A straight-jacket? *(They are all gone. Music. Prelude to* Das Rheingold.*)*

LISE. *Was* there too much ... what, *music...*? Even for the best of circumstances...?

AMALIA. Which these were not ...

LISE. Oh, don't get me wrong ...

LISE and AMALIA. ... it was a very happy home ...

LISE. It's just that ... something about the way they ... *saw* things ... was — wasn't — *(Music. Lights begin to change.)*

ACT ONE

Scene 1

In the dark, the "Magic Fire" music from the end of Die Walküre. *Lights up on a living room. A few pieces indicating an old-fashioned, middle-class, faded drawing room. Worn Persian rug, comfortable armchairs. There is an old, ornate upright piano in an odd position, isolated from the rest of the set, as if it were simultaneously nowhere and everywhere. Otto, in black tie, and Lise 2, on a wooden rocking horse, Valkyrie helmet (newspaper-made) on her head, in pajamas, listen to the phonograph. Muffled street noises.*

OTTO. *(As the music plays.)* ... and he kisses the godhead from his daughter's eyes and she falls into a deep sleep. He strikes the ground with his spear and from the center of the earth ...
LISE. *(Dovetailing.)* ... from the innermost corner of his heart ...
OTTO. ... he brings forth a magic fire that surrounds her in a blazing ring and burns through the darkness into infinite space ...
LISE 2. Why does he do that?
OTTO. To protect her from the dark forest.
LISE 2. Aren't they on top of a mountain?
OTTO. Yes, well, one finds dark forests everywhere. Now, this magic fire only a very great hero can cross.
LISE 2. What's a hero?
OTTO. A man who will go through the fire.
LISE 2. Does the magic fire burn?
OTTO. Only if you're afraid. So the father says: *(Otto speaks as the Wotan sings.)* "Whosoever fears the tip of this spear shall never pass through the fire." (The music takes over and for a moment high flickering flames dance on the living room walls and on the faces of both Lises who are transfixed.) And as the flames rage around his sleeping daughter, he turns and walks away.
LISE 2. *(Indignant.)* He leaves her there all alone? In the fire?

18

OTTO. He can't stay. Soon she'll be a woman. Mortal.

LISE 2. What's "mortal"? *(Amalia, in evening gown, enters, a wrap on one arm, gloves on the other, and takes the needle off the record. The spell is broken.)*

AMALIA. Don't make that fire too high, Otto. I want her married one day.

LISE. I was! Couple of times.

LISE 2. *(To Lise.)* You're kidding!

LISE. Shut up.

AMALIA. *(Setting her things down.)* The baby's asleep. Finally.

LISE 2 and LISE. *(Under their breath.)* Little creep.

AMALIA. It's your little brother!

LISE 2. *(Beat.)* How does he know she's in there, in the fire?

OTTO. Who?

LISE 2. The hero.

OTTO. He doesn't.

LISE 2. He just goes through fires looking for ladies?

OTTO. Aaahhh … well, yes and no …

LISE 2. Where do heroes live?

OTTO. *(Beat.)* I don't know.

LISE 2. Do I get to see one?

AMALIA. I hope so or there'll be hell to pay.

LISE. My mother always *could* foresee trouble ahead.

AMALIA. *(To Lise.)* Two divorces. Really. We *all* have lapses in taste, darling. We don't *marry* them.

OTTO. Heroes can be very frightening.

LISE 2. Why?

OTTO. They remind people of what they're not.

AMALIA. Homework, Lise.

LISE 2. Later.

AMALIA. Later you're going to bed. Now.

LISE 2. It only takes a second.

AMALIA. Go!

LISE 2. Fine. *(Lise 2 exits dragging her feet. Offstage.)* Hell.

AMALIA and OTTO. Mouth!

AMALIA. She doesn't fit in with other children, you know.

OTTO. I don't want her to *fit in*. Groups are what lynching mobs are made of.

LISE. For Papi, a mob was more than two people *not* gathered for the purposes of listening to music.

AMALIA. I want her to know the world as it *is,* not the Vienna

19

Philharmonic version. *(Outside, trucks drive by. The shouts "Perón! Perón! Perón!" are distantly heard. Otto closes the windows.)*

OTTO. Oh, *that,* out there ...

AMALIA. What's keeping Rosa, I wonder. Can't we ask Henri?

OTTO. How can I ask a man in his position to search the where-abouts of a missing plumber?

AMALIA. It's her brother.

OTTO. *(Beat.)* What time is it?

AMALIA. Going on seven. *(Elena enters, smart New Look suit, hat, gloves, etc., folded newspaper in hand.)*

ELENA. Hello darlings! The front door's open. You'll be murdered in your sleep.

AMALIA. There's only the Fontannes across the hall. They're taking us to the opera. Rosa's out and the doorbell's not working again.

OTTO. What's going on out there?

ELENA. Nothing. The usual. A truckload of strikebreakers going to work. Alberto here yet?

OTTO. No, is he coming over?

ELENA. He's picking me up here. We're going to the fights.

AMALIA. Since when do *you* go to the fights?

ELENA. He's hoping I'll find them inspiring. He says I'm dull as a spoon since I've been out of work. Actually I can't wait to see a couple of Perónist sons-of-bitches kick the shit out of each other.

AMALIA. Shhhh!

OTTO. *(Overlap.)* Cinzano?

ELENA. Please. Twist. Is the Black Widow going with you?

AMALIA. Lena! Your own grandmother. No wonder people talk about us.

LISE. / They do? They did?

ELENA. / *(Overlapping, to Otto.)* You've married into the House of Atreus, darling. The name Guarneri is only a smoke screen.

LISE. / *Who* talked about us?!

ELENA. / *(Lighting a cigarette.)* I brought you Alberto's editorial tonight. *(She opens the paper.)*

OTTO. Not about the strikes again.

ELENA. About *me!*

LISE. *(To audience.)* Nobody talked about us. *(To Amalia.)* What did they say?

ELENA. *(Reading.)* Here it is. Well, he says a lot of nice things, but here's the finish: "Elena Guarneri was *spectacular* in the *inexplicably* short run of *The House of Bernarda Alba* as the crippled Martirio.

20

That was three years ago. Surely her absence from our national theatre is her choice, but couldn't someone persuade her to return? We
seem to be misplacing all our important artists." Isn't that sweet?

AMALIA. I don't see why of all the parts you had to pick the
hunchback.

ELENA and LISE. Because it's the best one. *(Alberto enters.)*

ALBERTO. Why is your front door open?

ELENA.	AMALIA.	LISE.
Albertino!	Darling!	Alberto!

ALBERTO. Hello, beauties. *(He kisses Amalia and Elena.)*

AMALIA. Doorbell's broken. They're sending a man to fix it. Any
week now.

ALBERTO. *(Sharp.)* Don't use people you don't know. I'll send
you my handyman. Look at you! Where's everybody going?

AMALIA. To *Tosca*. We're waiting for Rosa.

ELENA. Where is she?

AMALIA. Gone to see about her brother.

ELENA. What about him?

OTTO. He's a plumber.

AMALIA. Hasn't been home in three days.

ALBERTO. Oh?

ELENA. Held prisoner by an amorous housewife? What … I give up.

ALBERTO. His union went on unauthorized strike a couple / of
days ago.

AMALIA. / *(Overlap and pressing.)* The usual?

ALBERTO. Please. *(Amalia starts his drink. Lise 2 appears.)*

LISE 2. Hi, Aunt Lena. Did you bring me truffles?

ELENA. No. I brought you a hug.

LISE 2. *(Gagging noise. To Alberto.)* You're not gonna hug me, are you?

ALBERTO. I'd sooner hug a black mamba.

LISE 2. Got anything good on you?

ALBERTO. *(Searching his pockets.)* How about some gum?

AMALIA. No gum. She's a young lady, not a camel. Back to
homework, Lise.

LISE 2. I finished.

AMALIA. Then go do your *solfège*.

LISE 2. I did it already!

AMALIA. Do it again.

LISE 2. *(On her way out, snorting.)* Hell.

OTTO, AMALIA, ELENA and ALBERTO. *(Automatically.)* Mouth!

AMALIA. *(To Otto, accusingly.)* She can only count in three-quarter time. It's disgraceful. *(Offstage, unintelligible grunts and assorted rude noises. Checking her watch.)* Aunt Paula's going to be late, of course.

ELENA. No, I passed her downstairs, chatting with the doorman.

ALBERTO. That man's a block "supervisor."

OTTO. What? We've known him for years!

AMALIA. *(Overriding Alberto and handing him the drink.)* Fernet and soda. What have you been doing with yourself?

ALBERTO. Nothing new. *(Lightly.)* Trying to keep the newspaper open, myself out of jail, that sort of thing. *(Pulling two paperbacks from his pocket.)* New Borges, new Cortázar, Lena.

ELENA. *(Grabbing them.)* Where did you get them?!

ALBERTO. Newspapermen have "ways and means" too, you know …

OTTO. Put them away. We're expecting people.

ELENA. You're going to the opera with them!

OTTO. Keep your voice down. *(Paula — a touch strangely dressed in a sari of sorts, and some runaway feathers — and Clara, in black and pearls, enter together.)*

CLARA. Good evening all. Look whom I rescued from the loquacious doorman.

PAULA. *(At the door.)* Ave!

CLARA. *Bon soir,* Lena.

ELENA. *Soir,* Clara. How are you finding the Plaza?

CLARA. Glum. It used to be one of the great hotels. What happened to the *thé dansant*s, the string quartets, the fresh flowers, the white gloves on the staff?

PAULA. They went the way of the generals.

CLARA. I'll never understand why one can't have a gracious democracy.

ALBERTO. Oh, you think this is a democ — ?

OTTO. Alberto, this is my mother's sister, Clara Stepaneck, visiting from Paris. Aunt Clara, Alberto Barcos, an old friend. Come give us a kiss, Paula. Sherry, ladies?

ALBERTO. *(Shaking hands.)* A pleasure.

PAULA. Just soda for me, dear. You know I don't have a head for wine.

ALBERTO. *(To Elena.)* We should go, Bugs.

ELENA. *(Putting on her gloves.)* How's the theatre in Paris these days, Clara?

CLARA. Also glum. We have a dreary Irishman writing in French. All the rage. Nobody knows *what* he's talking about. Two bums and a tree stump. All night. *Very* discouraging.

AMALIA. *(To Alberto and Elena.)* Aren't you going to be late? I wish Rosa would get here. We should go too. *(Alberto and Elena exit, noisily ad-libbing goodbyes.)*

ELENA. *(Offstage.)* / Is there lots of blood? It's not going to make me sick, is it? Violence has been known to make me sick.

ALBERTO. *(Offstage.)* Throwing up in public is *not* an option, Lena. Just so you know. You throw up on me, I don't know you.

AMALIA. / *(Overlap.)* Where's Nonna, Paula?

PAULA. Your father's bringing her. I'll call. *(Looking around.)* Where's the telephone?

AMALIA. The hallway.

PAULA. *(Exiting.)* What's the telephone doing in the hallway? *(Clara looks at Otto who looks away.)*

AMALIA. *(Exiting.)* Oh, people always jump when it rings and the *hors d'oeuvres* go flying. Mushrooms everywhere. *(Over their exit, Otto hands Clara a glass of sherry.)*

CLARA. Thank you. The telephone in the hallway? *(Beat.)* Everything all right?

OTTO. Oh, yes. Yes.

CLARA. I saw your mother in London. She's concerned.

OTTO. About what?

CLARA. She hears the situation here's turning — difficult?

OTTO. We're fine. Everything's fine.

CLARA. I'm to ask you all to come back with me if —

OTTO. It'll pass.

CLARA. This man next door, Paula says —

LISE. Ah ... yes ... *(Forgotten all about him ...)*

OTTO. Amalia's family is all here.

AMALIA. *(Entering with Paula.)* They're not coming. Nonna wants to go see a crucifixion movie.

OTTO. Another one?

AMALIA. It's a festival.

PAULA. Oh, Clara and I saw Angelica just outside. She says Henri may have to meet us at the theatre.

CLARA. The wife?

PAULA.	AMALIA.
Yes.	Beautiful woman.

CLARA. She wears her pearls too tight.

OTTO. I'll call a cab.

AMALIA. I don't have my violets.

23

PAULA. Send Rosa to the gypsy by the grocery store.

OTTO. *(On his way out.)* She's a Romanian Jew.

PAULA. She says she's a gypsy, and what people say about themselves is always truer than the truth, facts being, for the most part, completely unreliable. *(To Clara.)* Of course, with us there is always the spectacular factor. Our poor cousin Leila always said she wouldn't live past twenty-five, and on her twenty-fifth birthday, she ate a bagful of arsenic ... *(Lise mouths the words "bagful of arsenic" with Paula who moves around the room without settling anywhere for long.)*

CLARA. My word ... *(Lise 2 appears at the door and listens.)*

PAULA. Off to the apothecary she went, and bought herself a bag of arsenic — for the rats, she told poor Don Ramón who won't sell this family an aspirin since, and that was *years* ago — and swallowed it with her favorite Lapsang Souchong tea. I always preferred Oolong.

CLARA. How ... odd ...

PAULA. Not at all. The Windsors like it too.

CLARA. No, I mean, your unfortunate cousin ...

PAULA. Ah, yes. Well, nobody ever knew why. She *started off* with those disappointed eyes people usually *end up* with, you see, — some women *know* from the very beginning —

AMALIA. We're brooding!

PAULA. — and, of course, she had the family's penchant for extravagant behavior, but she was young, she was beautiful, she had —

AMALIA. — and we're going to hear such pretty music!

OTTO. *(Reentering.)* Oh, well, *Tosca* ...

CLARA. Too much Flaubert, I imagine.

PAULA. Oh, no, she only read comic books.

LISE 2. *(At the door.)* Cousin Leila was crazy too?

PAULA. What does she mean *"too"*?

AMALIA. What did I say about listening at doors?

LISE 2 and LISE. I want know what's going on.

OTTO. What are you, the KGB? *(Offstage door.)*

AMALIA. *(Crossing to the door quickly.)* Rosa, is that you?

ROSA. *(Offstage.)* Yes, Mrs. Berg.

AMALIA. / Oh, good. Did you — would you run downstairs and get a bunch of violets from Anya?

ROSA. *(Entering.)* Sure. Anything from the store?

AMALIA. No, thank you. *(Rosa exits.)*

LISE 2. / *(To Lise.)* How come these people never answer questions?

LISE. I know, it's awful.

LISE 2. Why'd she eat rat poison?

OTTO. Isn't it time she went to bed, or had her bath, or something?

AMALIA. Come along, dear.

LISE 2. It's early!

AMALIA. It's bed time.

LISE 2. Not in Tokyo! *(Amalia exits with Lise 2. Offstage.)* It's unfair! / How come Cousin Leila ate rat poison?

AMALIA. *(Offstage.)* She was a brooder ...

OTTO. / *(Overlap.)* Paula, I think Lise's a little young to —

PAULA. *(Gaily.)* Bound to know sooner or later. No use finding out about your relatives too late to make a clean getaway. *(To Clara.)* Not that anyone ever *has* ... save Leila ...

OTTO. May I freshen up your — your soda water, Paula?

PAULA. This family ... Have to be bloody *Houdini.* Ha-ha! *(Confidentially.)* We're not as hospitable as we may seem —

OTTO. Oh God ...

PAULA. — at first glimpse ... *(She winks disconcertingly at Clara.)*

OTTO. *(Calling.)* Amalia! *(Offering a bowl to Clara.)* Nuts!

CLARA. Who...?

OTTO. No, do you —

PAULA. *(Trying to get it all in before Amalia returns.)* And there was my poor uncle Peruccio, too, you know. Another casualty.

OTTO. — want some —

PAULA. A heart surgeon.

OTTO. — nuts ... *(Amalia enters. Otto makes wild head signals towards Paula.)*

PAULA. He turns fifty and he announces — with his last gasp of youth — that he's always wanted to be a painter. The wife and the sons become hysterical. Slits his own throat.

CLARA. / Goodness ...

LISE. / So much for the sunny Italians ...

AMALIA. Paula! How can you! You know very well Peruccio didn't kill himself!

PAULA. Well, because he botched it, which was so clumsy. It made him very awkward to sit across from at the dinner table. One was always *looking.*

OTTO. A little more sherry, Aunt Clara?

PAULA. *(Vaguely.)* Blood all over the wallpaper.

CLARA. *(To Otto.)* Please!

PAULA. Like a splash of those red poppies he painted for years afterwards locked up in the attic in the middle of the night.

AMALIA. *(A strained smile.)* Really, Paula ... *(Sotto voce.)* Pills, darling!

LISE. / Pills...?

PAULA. / Needless to say, people no longer trust him with their hearts. *(Sternly, to Lise.)* Let that be a lesson to you! *(On her way to her purse for the pillbox, she notices the rocking horse. Formally.)* Hello.

OTTO. *(To Paula.)* Aunt Clara doesn't know you all very well yet, dear. What is she going to think? *(To Clara.)* It's a very large family. Many of them — *most*, in fact, are quite — normal. It's just that Paula only likes the crazy ones.

PAULA. What crazy ones? *Some* have a healthily metaphorical approach to life, that's all.

OTTO. People aren't interesting only when they're committing suicide!

PAULA. *(To Clara.)* Dullness is so often confused with sanity. *(Under this Otto busies himself with the sherry. Paula discreetly pulls out a tiny pill box from her purse and takes one. Rosa enters and crosses to Amalia. They are at some distance from the others who chat.)*

LISE. *(To Paula, re the pills.)* What are those?

PAULA. Wings ...

ROSA. She had no violets left. Somebody bought her out.

AMALIA. How thoughtless. *(Quietly.)* Any news?

ROSA. *(Idem.)* Not yet.

AMALIA. He'll turn up. Would you see to Lise? She's overexcited.

ROSA. Well, of course. *(A malevolent look at Paula.)* Loons running about the house babbling God knows what day and night. *(Exits muttering.)* Cracked. Every one of 'em ...

PAULA. *(To Clara.)* People must put themselves to good use. And we don't.

LISE. *I* did! I do ... don't I?

PAULA. Not a single one of us. Cousin Boccio wanted to sing. Beautiful voice. Like Malia's ...

LISE. *(Surprised, to Amalia.)* Did you, really?

AMALIA. *(Sharply.)* Paula harbors the romantic idea that this is a family of failed artists.

LISE. *(An old grudge.)* You never thought we were special.

AMALIA. It was a very happy house! Lots of girls.

LISE. *Girls* ... you always said "girls."

AMALIA. My first memories are of a houseful of girls and music.

Guitars and violins at midnight in the patio, jasmine and gardenia in bloom, and girls making music, laughing …

PAULA. … swallowing poison …

AMALIA. *(An edge.)* Maybe Peruccio's poppies and Boccio's voice weren't any good after all. There's always *that* possibility.

PAULA. *(Peevish.)* We'll never know now, will we? *(To no one in particular.)* Dandelions in a gale … I should have run away. *(Otto pours himself a cognac.)*

OTTO. And done what, Paula?

PAULA. … Dance …

OTTO. Dance! Really? Like Isadora Duncan?

PAULA. Oh, no, dear. Like Pavlova. *(To Clara.)* I saw her when I was a little girl. She's not dancing, she's dreaming up there, I thought. And right away I wanted — After all, there isn't all that much to be said for being *relentlessly* awake, now is there … Ha-ha! But Mother … *(Pause.)* Anna Pavlova, silent and white, rose *en pointe* towards the night and vanquished it. The bloom of a cloud. The crest of a wave … Oh, dear, the best memory of my youth is that of a performance. I'm sure there's something very wrong with that.

LISE. Why didn't you?

PAULA. What?

LISE. Dance.

PAULA. No nerve. *(Henri Fontannes enters in civilian clothes, an armful of violets. The general tone abruptly goes "up." Otto and Amalia ad-lib greetings a little too brightly.)*

HENRI. Make room, make room!

LISE. Who — *(Vaguely remembering.)* Oh … right…!

HENRI. *(Overlap.)* The first violets of winter, for the beautiful Guarneri girls. *(He distributes bouquets.)*

AMALIA. Henri, how lovely! And so many!

PAULA. The perfume…!

AMALIA. So *you're* the one — I'll get a bowl. Vermouth? Otto, pour Henri a quick vermouth, no ice, no twist, and we'll be off. *(She exits.)*

HENRI. A small one, please. I have to go back to the office.

OTTO. At this hour? What about *Tosca*?

HENRI. I'm sorry. Budgets and balances, all that interesting stuff.

OTTO. Aunt Clara, this is Henri Fontannes, our next-door neighbor, whose box at the opera we're using tonight. Henri, my aunt, Clara Stepaneck, just arrived from Paris.

HENRI. Ah, our sister-city. Mrs. Stepaneck, how do you do.

(Offering her a small bunch.) Will you accept a few violets from a stranger?

CLARA. *(Delighted, taking the flowers.)* You're very kind.

HENRI. That's a — uh — a stunning dress, Paula.

PAULA. It's a copy of a ceremonial *sari*. For *suttee*. *(Amalia enters with a crystal bowl. She has pinned some violets to her shoulder and arranges the remaining ones in the bowl.)*

HENRI. / For what?

PAULA. *Suttee.* That's when the Hindu widows throw themselves — or are *pushed* — onto their husbands' funeral pyres.

OTTO. They haven't done that in a century!

PAULA. Pity. *(To Clara.)* In this country, women with no husbands are buried alive with their mothers.

AMALIA. I'm afraid Paula is obsessed with self-destruction today.

OTTO. Here you are. *(He hands Henri a glass of vermouth.)*

HENRI. Thank you. The violets are by way of apology. I can't go tonight.

AMALIA. Oh, no, why?

HENRI. Meetings, what else? Nobody told me this job meant morning to midnight meetings. I used to have a life. But: That's what I have to look forward to this evening, instead of the balm of friendship and lovely music.

OTTO. Oh, well, *Tosca* ...

HENRI. Angelica's beginning to call herself "the widow Fontannes" and to accept condolence visits. Thank you for keeping her company, by the way.

AMALIA. We'll try our best to stop her from considering new marriage proposals. *(Lise 2 appears with a book under her arm in bunny slippers with tire-track marks across them.)*

LISE 2. Uncle H! / Bring me any truffles?

LISE. / *Uncle H* ...

HENRI. Who's my best buddy?!

LISE 2. *(Running to him.)* Me!

LISE. *(Distanced.)* Really?

HENRI. As it happens, I know people in the chocolate contraband business. *(He pulls a handful of chocolate truffles out of his pocket, gives them to Lise 2 and takes her book. They sit side by side.)* Dr. Jekyll and Mr. Hyde? Before bed?

OTTO. *(Pointedly.)* She takes books from the shelves without asking.

LISE 2. Are you gonna go see the "toss-the-baby-in-the-fire" thing?

OTTO. It's called *Il Trovatore* and no, we're seeing the "pitch-the-lady-off-the-tower" thing.

LISE 2. Oh, *Tosca*. Too much kissing. *(Gagging sounds. Then to Henri.)* I'm going to *La Traviata* next week.

HENRI. Don't you think this kid's getting too much opera?

OTTO. I don't want her to grow up thinking opera's an elite affair attended by stuffy old bores. It's rowdy good fun!

HENRI. Otto, please: Lucia murders her husband and goes barking mad. Tosca jumps off a tower after stabbing a man to death. Butterfly slashes her own throat, Senta hurls herself into the sea, Leonora takes poison, Norma and Brünhilde *both* walk into raging fires, one escorted by her boyfriend, the other by her favorite pet …

OTTO, LISE 2, LISE and PAULA. Fun!

HENRI. Hardly encouraging examples for a growing girl!

LISE. Needless to say, I had already developed a pathological aversion to the ordinary.

AMALIA. She's started to bite.

LISE and LISE 2. *(Belligerent.)* Who says?

HENRI. You see?

CLARA. Just like Otto when he was a little boy.

HENRI. Did you know your front door's open?

OTTO. For you.

LISE 2. What's *La Traviata* about? *(Deadly silence. Then all the women stampede out of the room.)*

WOMEN. *(Ad libs.)* Oh, I left — / There's a draft — / Goodness, where is — / Look at my hair! / I *must* powder my mouth — my *nose!* / Excuse me.

HENRI. *(To Otto.)* I rest my case.

LISE 2. *(Nosing interesting information.)* So what's it about?

OTTO. OK. Say good night, Lise.

LISE 2. *(Outraged.)* What?! Why?!

OTTO. Because I'm your father and I say so.

LISE 2. That's unfair!

AMALIA. *(Entering.)* Say good night, Lise.

LISE 2. Every time — *(Amalia whisks Lise 2 offstage. From offstage:)* What about the *Traviata* lady?

AMALIA. *(Offstage.)* She wasn't a lady, dear.

LISE 2. *(Offstage.)* What *was* she?!

AMALIA. *(Offstage.)* A working girl …

LISE 2. *(Offstage.)* I DON'T WANNA GO TO BED!

AMALIA. *(Offstage.)* You'll wake up the baby!

LISE 2. *(Offstage.)* Little creep. *(Pause.)*

OTTO. I think they make her braids too tight.

HENRI. You know anybody who can use my seat?

OTTO. Not at this hour.

HENRI. Well, good night.

OTTO. *(Walking him out.)* Any news on Mrs. Perón's condition?

HENRI. She won't last the month. *(Beat.)* Seen Alberto lately?

OTTO. You just missed him. He's taken Lena to the fights.

HENRI. Always did love a fight, Alberto. *(Beat.)* We used to be such good friends. At university.

OTTO. Ah, yes, he mentioned …

HENRI. *(Pleased.)* Did he? Best buddies. I don't see him much any more.

OTTO. He's very busy with the paper.

HENRI. Yes. *(Beat.)* Those editorials of his are … He's making things terribly difficult for himself. *(A nervous laugh.)* As always. *(Tentative.)* Also, the recent enforcement of Article 2H —

OTTO. Article 2H …

HENRI. Of Regulations for Procedures against Criminal Behavior. It concerns — homosexuals among other things. Tell him.

OTTO.	LISE.
(Beat.) Alberto?	What…?

HENRI. *(Embarrassed.)* You didn't know? I didn't mean to — Well, good night again. I *am* sorry about tonight. *(Rosa enters from the kitchen.)*

ROSA. It started to rain. *(Amalia, Paula, and Clara enter, gathering their wraps, putting on gloves, etc. Paula, Clara and Otto start to exit with Henri. Lise 2 appears dragging a large headless doll in a red dress.)*

LISE 2. *(To Henri.)* Marie-Antoinette wants you to read to her.

OTTO. Uncle H has to go back to work, Lise.

HENRI. I can read to Mme. Defarge for a few minutes. *(Exiting with Lise 2.)* But I'm not reading any *Jekyll and Hyde*. I want to be able to sleep nights. *(Henri and Lise 2 exit into the house, Otto and the others go into the hallway. Amalia and Rosa stay behind.)*

LISE 2. *(Offstage.)* / What d'you wanna read?

HENRI. *(Offstage.)* The *Peter Pan* I gave you last week?

LISE 2. *(Offstage.)* The little creep that flies into people's bedrooms? Awww …

HENRI. *(Offstage.)* How about *The Flying Dutchman* then?

LISE 2. *(Offstage.)* Who's that?

HENRI. *(Offstage.)* Once upon a time there was a ghost ship …

AMALIA. / *(Overlap.)* Make sure Lise goes to bed early, Rosa.

ROSA. Won't do any good. She'll be up half the night. I say filling her head with music about screaming women on flying horses is not good for the nerves.

AMALIA. I tell him every day. *(Quickly, quietly.)* What did they say about your brother?

ROSA. *(Idem.)* Nothing. They never heard of 'im. That kinda thing. One guy laughed, another one checked my papers ... They asked me why I wasn't registered with the CGT. My name is on some list now.

AMALIA. A formality, I'm sure.

ROSA. Strikes are legal, aren't they?

AMALIA. I — not all of them, I hear.

ROSA. Always changin' the rules on you. It's hard to keep up, you know? I thought these guys was *for* the working man.

AMALIA. Maybe they just want to talk to him. Nothing serious.

ROSA. Why would they say they don't have him then?

AMALIA. People don't just — *disappear,* Rosa.

ROSA. I'm scared, Mrs. Berg.

AMALIA. Of what?

ROSA. That's the thing! I don't know! Everything. Little things: the telephone, the doorbell, a guy on the corner, the doorman ... All these *lists* you gotta be on or not be on. Santo's not a criminal. He works hard all week, weekends he plays soccer. That's it. That's his life. *(Beat.)* 'Course he wants to play for the World Cup one day ... Santo Arrúa: goalie! All over the papers! Head-in-the-clouds-Santo, we call 'im. Eddy, that's his buddy, he says to 'im, he says: "Santo, you gotta keep your eye on the ball, kid. You always thinkin' of somethin' else out there!" *(Beat.)* See that's what I'm worried about. Maybe ... he thought 'imself into some kinda trouble? *(Beat.)* He's only twenty-four. *(Otto puts his head in.)*

OTTO. Cab's here.

AMALIA. Coming. *(To Rosa.)* I'm sure he'll turn up, Rosa. Good night. Don't wait up.

ROSA. He had a mole on his left cheek.

AMALIA. Who?

ROSA. The guy that laughed at me. A reddish kind of mole. I'd recognize him anywhere. Years from now. *(Amalia exits.)*

LISE. I didn't know you had a brother ...

ROSA. Yes you did. He made you a paper boat once, remember? With red sails and a black mast ... A ghost ship ... *(Rosa exits.)*

LISE. A ghost ship ... *(Music: the distant, eerie horn call of* The

31

Flying Dutchman. *Abruptly.*) I don't remember that … *(Lise 2 appears in her pajamas, using a tablecloth as some sort of costume, rushes to the phonograph, puts on a record at an ear-splitting level. The end of* Tosca. *She climbs on the couch and lip-synchs to the soprano. Rosa comes back in, attracted by the noise.)*
TOSCA.
    O SCARPIA! AVANTI A DIO!
(And with the grand finale she hurls herself to the ground where she crawls around making various and extended agonic noises and ending up sprawled "dead" on the carpet with her tongue hanging out, looking something like roadkill. Rosa stares grimly at Lise.)
LISE. What…?

Scene 2

Next day. Late afternoon. Otto and Henri sit with coffee, cognac and cigarettes.

HENRI. And how was the opera?
OTTO. Sung at no risk. I could have stayed home and played the record. And your meeting?
HENRI. I now have an officious little Pygmy named Alfonso, as "budget secretary" who lives to terrorize me. They know I'm interested in social reform, not in balancing ledgers, and they send me this imbecile — *(Amalia enters followed by Rosa.)*
AMALIA. Lise's school bus was stopped. They took the driver and one of the nuns.

HENRI.	OTTO.
Who did?	What?

ROSA. *(Cautiously.)* Trouble with the church again.
OTTO. Just now?
AMALIA. Your daughter bit one of the soldiers.
OTTO. *Soldiers?* On a school bus?
AMALIA. National Guard.
HENRI. *(Under his breath.)* / *Goddamn it!*
ROSA. / They were yanking chains off the kids' necks. One of them grabbed her medal of the Holy Virgin, and she almost took

two of his fingers off.

LISE. He grabbed me! He put his hand right here, and —

ROSA. Sister Raymondis is scared to death.

OTTO. What in hell —

LISE. — *he grabbed me!*

ROSA. Regular barracuda.

LISE. Dirty nails ... taste of / metal ...

ROSA. / *(Overlap.)* Blood. She drew blood.

LISE. This didn't happen — / *all* the time —

OTTO. / Where is she?

AMALIA. Sitting in the kitchen, poor little thing ...

ROSA. ... stuffing her face ...

AMALIA. She kept her medal but the nuns don't want to bring her home any more.

ROSA. *(To Otto.)* They want you to pick her up after school.

OTTO. She *bit* a man?

HENRI. Good girl!

OTTO. What's this all about?

HENRI. The driver must have been under some sort of — of investigation ...

OTTO. For what?

HENRI. Who knows! The incompetence — Nobody checks with anybody, people go off half-cocked. It's a goddamn mess up there!

OTTO. Where ...

HENRI. Good thing they caught up with him. Driving a busload of little girls, for godsakes. I need to use the phone.

OTTO. It's in the hallway.

HENRI. I don't want to tie up your line.

OTTO. Leave the door open.

LISE. It was always open to him ... always ... *(Henri starts out as Lise 2 enters eating a huge slice of bread and jam which is all over her face.)*

OTTO. Lise!

HENRI. *(Kneeling next to her.)* You all right, princess?

LISE 2. *(Mouth full.)* Uh-huh.

HENRI. Nobody hurt you? You tell Uncle H, now.

LISE 2. Nah. Anita D'Angelo puked. And Heidi Bleiman peed *all over*.

AMALIA. That's nice, dear. We won't go *on and on* about it, though. *(They check her for signs of bodily and mental harm, none of which she displays. Henri exits.)*

LISE 2. Can I go play outside?

33

OTTO. No!

LISE 2. *(Gleeful.)* You have to pick me up from school now.

OTTO. I want to.

LISE 2. *(Beat. Mouth still full.)* I don't feel so good …

AMALIA. It's her nerves!

ROSA. It's the four pieces of bread and jam and two cups of hot chocolate with whipped cream.

LISE 2. … I'm gonna be sick …

AMALIA. Well, of course, the shock …

ROSA. The mouth! Come along, Lise.

LISE 2. *(On their way out.)* I'm gonna die …

ROSA. You're not. That guy's gonna die.

LISE 2. *(Weakly.)* What guy?

ROSA. The guy you bit. *(She takes Lise 2 who exits moaning.)*

OTTO. *(Beat.)* I feel like we're stumbling through a mine field.

LISE. / It wasn't like that …

AMALIA. / *(Overlap.)* We don't know what actually happened yet.

LISE. Exactly!

OTTO. Amalia, please. *(Henri enters.)* That was quick.

HENRI. It seems the man was involved in some kind of smuggling operation with Brazil — do you have a cigarette? I'm out — *(Otto gives him one.)* the usual stuff, proscribed goods, etc.

OTTO. I see. *(Lights his cigarette, watches him.)* And the nun?

HENRI. Unfortunately, the woman was involved with him.

AMALIA. A nun?

HENRI. It's simple enough. A young woman who happens to be a nun meets a young man and … naturally …

AMALIA. What's going to happen to her?

HENRI. I couldn't tell you. I'm sure the sisters don't want her around the girls anymore. They'll probably send her away somewhere. To another convent.

OTTO. And the driver?

HENRI. Spend some time in jail, I hope.

OTTO. They were tearing medals and crosses off their necks, Henri. *Little girls.*

HENRI. Inexcusable. I've told them a thousand times not to use the army for standard police work. Clods!

AMALIA and LISE. *(Softly.)* You've told them?

HENRI. *(Laughs.)* I wouldn't worry too much, though. Far as I can tell *these* little girls chewed up, peed on and got sick all over a platoon of large men in riot gear who seemed to be heavily on the losing side.

34

AMALIA. It's ... unsettling.

HENRI. Yes, well. That's what you get when you send your daughter to a school run by unmarried women. Chaos. Damn, look at the time. Angelica's expecting me. Don't worry. Really.

OTTO. Thank you.

HENRI. Not at all. You think she's all right then?

AMALIA. She's fine. I'll walk you out. *(Amalia and Henri exit talking. Rosa enters to clear the coffee table. Otto lights a cigarette.)*

AMALIA. *(Offstage.)* Are you interested in seeing the Russians dance?

HENRI. *(Offstage.)* Always. When are they coming?

AMALIA. *(Offstage.)* / Next month, looks like. *Sleeping Beauty.*

HENRI. *(Offstage.)* Angelica will love it.

ROSA. / *(Over the above.)* Mr. Berg?

OTTO. Oh, Rosa, leave that. I'll take care of it.

ROSA. Sir ...

OTTO. Yes?

ROSA. That nun? Sister Clotilde? She's not that kind.

OTTO. What kind?

ROSA. *That* kind. What he said. She's a plain little thing. Not likely to be —

OTTO. Now, Rosa, plainer women than that have —

ROSA. Not her. You can tell. *(Pause.)* Mr. Fontannes now — well, look at the way he finds out about things, so quick ... You think he could find out about Santo? Maybe put in a word?

OTTO. Oh, I don't know, Rosa. It's — He — it's just a desk job, he has ...

ROSA. But in the — with the government, right?

OTTO. Ah ... yes, but I'm not sure exactly what —

ROSA. Could you ask him then? I'd be grateful.

OTTO. I'd have to find the right — I'll do my best.

ROSA. Thank you.

OTTO. Of course. *(Otto puts out his cigarette, crosses to the piano and with one finger picks out a few bars of* Ride of the Valkyries. *In a flash the door is open and Lise 2 pads in.)*

LISE 2. Is that the Valkyries, Papi?

OTTO. *(Absently.)* The Valkyries taking the / dead heroes —

LISE. *(Overlapping.)* — / dead heroes to Valhalla on horses made of storm clouds and smoke. *(Otto continues picking notes on the keyboard.)*

LISE 2.• They have horses that fly in the theatre?

LISE. Nowhere else. *(Amalia enters, newspaper in hand. Otto stops playing.)*

AMALIA. Lise, Rosa's running a bath for you.

LISE 2. When is Sister Clotilde coming back?

OTTO. *(Beat.)* Any day soon.

AMALIA. Go wash up for supper.

LISE 2. Hell. *(Shuffling off.)* I'm gonna be like *La Traviata* when I grow up. *(Offstage.)* A working girl.

OTTO.	AMALIA.
(Overlap.) GOOD GOD!	YOU SEE?!

LISE 2. *(Back at door.)* What'd I *say*?!

OTTO. Go take your bath!

LISE 2. *(Offstage.)* Fine.

AMALIA. Choke to death if she didn't have the last word. *(Silence.)*

OTTO. Did you find it convincing?

AMALIA. What …

OTTO. The driver … the nun … the —

AMALIA. It's over now. *(Opening a window.)* Beautiful evening. For June. I've got the dates for the Bolshoi here. They —

OTTO. It's happening all over again …

AMALIA. *(Exiting, reading the newspaper.)* Don't be silly. This is America. I wonder if they're bringing Plisitskaya … *(Otto smokes by a window, looking out at the Buenos Aires skyline. It's darker now. Lise 2 appears phone in hand.)*

LISE 2. *(Sotto voce.)* Hello? Is this Marco Dormanowicz? This is the Orphanage for Polish War Children. The woman you *think* is your mother is bringing you over tomorrow.

LISE and LISE 2. Pack your bags! *(Lise 2 hangs up. They shriek with laughter. Lise 2 scampers off into the dark. Lise is about to follow and is stopped by Otto. Lights change.)*

OTTO. *(Looking out the window.)* Did you know your great-uncle Heinrich was great friends with Wittgenstein?

LISE. No …

OTTO. Very funny man …

LISE. Who…?

OTTO. *(Still looking out the window.)* Your great-uncle …

LISE. *(Uneasily.)* Someone's … roaming the house … Who is — Who *was* that? *(Lise 2 has reappeared in the doorway dragging her headless doll.)*

LISE 2. Cousin Leila …

OTTO. There are no ghosts in this house, *liebschen.* Come, I'll show you. *(He picks her up and they exit singing Danilo's song from*

The Merry Widow.)
OTTO and LISE 2.
Da geh' ich zu Maxim,
dort bin ich sehr intim,
ich duze alle Damen,
ruf' sie beim Kosenamen …
(Offstage, Lise 2 and Otto are heard singing very distantly now.
Onstage, Lise chuckles softly and continues humming the song.)
LISE.   LoLo, DoDo, JouJou … (… *which peters out into an*
uncomfortable silence.) Where is everybody? Where did all the fun
people go? *(Otto and Lise 2 laugh offstage. She whistles some more.)*
So dark, all of a sudden. How did it get so dark? *(To the booth.)* Can
I have more light? *(Lights don't change.)* Hello! More light?
(Nothing.) Hell. *(She lights a cigarette and simultaneously, a shadow*
by the window does the same. In the flash of the lighter we see Henri's
face for a fraction of a second. Panic.) Papi?! *(From very far away, the*
eerie horn call from The Flying Dutchman.)

End of Act One

ACT TWO

Music: "Brindisi" from Traviata. *A Callas version. Night. A spot on Lise.*

LISE. June twenty-fourth, the feast of St. John, or *La Saint-Jean. Walpurgisnacht.* My birthday. For a while we had balloons and streamers and party hats ... We even had a magician once but ... somebody frightened him. And then one day, birthdays became strictly family affairs, no friends, no outsiders. The doors were shut and the music turned up. *(The entire family. Under the scene there is to be a constant ad-lib "track" of dialogue referring to the actual mechanics of eating, "pass the salt," etc. They're at the pâté and already shouting.)*

JUAN. Now Gigli, Muzio, Schipa —

MADDALENA. / *Un porco fascista,* Schipa!

JUAN. / — Tagliavini, they open the mouth, and sunshine comes out. Sun and the perfume of ripe, deep purple grapes. The Germans, they open the mouth, and out comes *chalk!* It dries the bones to hear it.

OTTO. *Chalk!?* Schwarzkopf, *chalk?* Lehmann, Jeritza, Windgassen, Wunderlich, *chalk?* We're talking about a voice, not a gush of syrup, Juan!

AMALIA. The new Greek woman, what's her name ...

MADDALENA. *(Deafly.)* Who?

AMALIA. *(Louder.)* The Greek! Soprano!

MADDALENA. *(Beat.)* Big girl.

AMALIA. What's her name ...

ELENA. She's American.

OTTO. She's Greek.

PAULA. She's scary.

JUAN. The Americans can't sing.

OTTO. Ponselle, Traubel, Farrar, Tibbett, Merrill ...

ALBERTO. Frank Sinatra ...

OTTO. Who?

MADDALENA. Italian boy.

JUAN. La Tebaldi, now ...

38

MADDALENA. Her too ...

JUAN. What ...

MADDALENA. What ...

JUAN. *(Louder.)* Her too *what?* Italian?

MADDALENA. *(Shouting.)* Big!

JUAN. Voice like an angel.

CLARA. Such a nice woman, Tebaldi.

ELENA. Who wants "nice" on stage? "Nice" is deadly. I'm never "nice" on stage.

JUAN. Well, naturally. Whoever heard of a nice actress?

LISE. Now just a minute — !

PAULA. You're an *actress?!*

LISE. Yes.

PAULA. How wonderful ...

OTTO. Artists are *terrible* people. It's we amateurs who are nice. *(The beginnings of a disturbance outside. The volume in the room increases.)*

ELENA. "Nice" is for bunny rabbits. *(Otto shuts the window. Outside noises are muted.)*

OTTO. "Nice art"! What's "nice art"? Art's life. "Nice" is entertainment. *(He draws the heavy double drapes shut and sits back down at the table.)*

AMALIA. There are people with perfectly nice lives.

PAULA. Who?

MADDALENA. Where?

CLARA. Really?

ELENA. Ha!

OTTO. Exactly.

JUAN. Nonsense. Life isn't nice or not nice, it just *is.* You ask from it what it can give, and it's all right. You ask for the moon, it's a different story. But then it's your fault. Measure is everything, no, Alberto?

ALBERTO. I don't always know what that measure is.

JUAN. It's what makes you get out of the way of a moving truck.

ELENA. No, that's common sense.

PAULA. *(To Alberto.)* You want to watch that, dear. You don't want to be taken for an accountant.

JUAN. I'm talking about measure; knowing how far to go and when to stop. *(To Alberto.)* You understand me?

OTTO. Well now, that's problematic. If Wagner had cared about "measure" he'd have never composed *The Ring.*

JUAN. Please. Sixteen ear-shattering hours about a one-eyed pyro-maniac with family problems? I say "measure" would have been of use. Don't change the subject. *(To Alberto.)* I have a right, you know. You're my godson. I watched you grow up.

ALBERTO. Are you telling me to be careful, *padrino?*

JUAN. I've a right! I took you to your first soccer game, I taught you to shave, I taught you to fight, I taught you to — Look: I want for you to sit in the sun — not too long — have a little wine — not too much — a little music — not too sad, none of that German stuff — a good wife, a couple of nice fat children and—

EVERYBODY. — and keep away from moving trucks! *(They laugh.)*

JUAN. ALL RIGHT! So I'm telling you to be careful! *(Silence.)* You're a picture-straightener, Albertino. And an ashtray-emptier. Since you were this tall. And now you want to take out the *trash.* And this worries me. You watch yourself. *(Awkwardly.)* All the men in your family: your father, your grandfather — all dead, son. *(An afterthought.)* Rest in peace. So … now you got nothing to prove. Not to me, not to anybody.

AMALIA. *(Changing the subject.)* You don't find art entertaining, Otto?

ELENA. Hell, the Sistine Chapel's a riot. *(Amalia laughs.)*

MADDALENA. *(Somber, to Juan.)* They make fun of Vatican? The actress and the actress's sister?

JUAN. Nobody make fun of the Vatican, *Mamma.*

ELENA. How come she hears every goddamn word *I* say?

JUAN. Amalia, Lena! *(To Maddalena.)* And they're your *grand-daughters,* remember?

MADDALENA. I not have granddaughters who go to work after the sun go down.

ELENA. I do matinées!

AMALIA. *(Overriding.)* More *pâté* anybody?

PAULA. Do you know *how* they get *pâté de foie-gras?*

AMALIA. Can opener…?

PAULA. They stick the poor goose in the ground — *in* it, you understand, then they push a tube down its poor neck —

OTTO. Amalia …

AMALIA. Auntie Paula, I don't think this is quite / the time to —

LISE 2. / *(Top of her lungs.)* And — and — they stuff things down 'im and get him sick and his liver gets all boogery and yellow and — and — it blows up! *(Disgusting wet exploding noises.)* And that's what you're eating. *(Beat. Elena precipitously leaves the room.)* It's pukey. *(Eyes stray over to Paula.)*

PAULA. Children should be well-informed. And it's hypocritical for carnivores to be squeamish.

OTTO. *Na, ja …*

ALBERTO. Sort of like political indoctrination for the masses. Get them good and stuck, and stuff garbage down their throats.

JUAN. Don't start. *(A police siren roars by.)*

CLARA. *(A little loud.)* Anybody been to the *Parsifal* yet?

JUAN. Ah, no, *cara*. That, no. Five hours of redemption. No. The *Pope* couldn't take it.

MADDALENA. Gianni!

AMALIA. Don't say "Pope" at the table, Papa. *(Elena enters, handkerchief to her mouth.)*

ELENA. Is she still here?

LISE 2. It's my birthday!

ELENA. Shakespeare died on his birthday, did you know, little girl?

ALBERTO. *(To Amalia.)* What's wrong with "Pope"?

ELENA. The present one was a Nazi.

OTTO. / He was not!

AMALIA. / *(Overlap.)* No politics and no religion, please!

JUAN. And I am not "Gianni" anymore, I am "Juan," *Mamma.* *(He pronounces it "Kuan")* How many times I have to tell you?

MADDALENA. Who's "Juan"? *(She also says "Kuan.")* I don't know "Juan." "Juan" is a stranger. The priest pour holy water on your bald head and call you "Gianni" *(She hits him on the back of the head.)* for the Lord and for your father and "Gianni" you stay. *(She hits him again.)* Who's "Juan"?

PAULA. More wine, mother?

MADDALENA. Again? What is this, a tavern? *(Rosa comes in and serves the soup.)*

AMALIA. *(Sotto.)* Any news?

ROSA. No. *(She goes around the table.)*

MADDALENA. Soup's for children. Where's the *gnocchi?*

ROSA. *(Muttering.)* Upside your head one of these days.

MADDALENA. Who is that?

AMALIA. You know perfectly well —

MADDALENA. *(To Juan.)* We not change name because we come to America! Your father said only for a little while. Then we go back. / Instead he plop down dead. ON PURPOSE!

JUAN. / Here we go …

ELENA. His only way out, poor man.

41

JUAN. Lena!

MADDALENA. *(Pointing to her heart.)* Il cuore. Always let you down.

PAULA. Only if you have one. *(A door buzzer in back.)*

AMALIA. Is that the service door, Rosa?

ROSA. Tomorrow's groceries. They work late. *(She exits.)*

MADDALENA. Welcher. I not know many words *not* in Italian. *Ma: steerage* was the first. Three weeks. With foreigners. Nobody ask me. I was *kidnappèd.*

OTTO. Sicilians and Neapolitans are Italians too, Nonna.

MADDALENA. Not where *I* come from.

JUAN. *(Sadly.)* They don't speak the language of Dante, Otto.

PAULA. And they scream in the streets. In their underwear.

MADDALENA. Welcher.

JUAN. Why you talk like that? You loved Papa.

MADDALENA. I not remember love. I remember *steerage.*

PAULA. Give her a little Marsala. *(Loud.)* Have a little Marsala, Mother.

MADDALENA. No! And don't touch alla time! I am not a crippled! And you know what else? I not make arrangement for my funeral in this country. You not take me back to Piemonte, you have big problem! I lie here unburied! I *ROT* in your living room and nobody get my money!

ELENA.	JUAN.
That's it. I'm going home.	Shoot me. Somebody shoot me.

AMALIA. Sit down. You're making her nervous.

ELENA. *I* make her nervous? *(Short outburst of distant unrest.)*

PAULA. Maybe a little bicarbonate of soda. *(She exits to the kitchen.)*

ALBERTO. It sounds kind of rough out there.

ELENA. What is it? *(They both go to the window and part the drapes.)*

ALBERTO. Police.

ELENA. Where?

ALBERTO. Unmarked cars. Look.

AMALIA. Close the drapes, please. Sit down. Pour Alberto some Chianti, Elena. I think that Bordeaux's a little acid.

ALBERTO. *(Still at window.)* They're looking for someone …

OTTO. What, around here? It's a very quiet neighborhood. *(Paula returns with a tall glass of bubbling bicarbonate and puts it in front of her mother with a shaky hand. She looks frightened.)*

PAULA. *(Pours herself a full glass of wine.)* Let's toast!

ELENA and LISE. Let's!

JUAN. Paula, you don't drink! Sit down, please! *(Sotto to Amalia.)*

42

Is she...? *(He mimes drinking.)*

PAULA. *(In a panic, toasting.)* To all foolish old maids who might have been Shakespeare's sister. *Salute! (She weeps. / Lise toasts, pours wine for all, gets involved with the Alberto-Otto conversation and does not hear the other exchange.)*

ALL.
/ *Salute! Prosit!*

ALBERTO.
Shakespeare had a sister?

OTTO.
We don't know this in Vienna.

ELENA.
Read your Virginia Woolf.

LISE.
You read Virginia Woolf?

LISE.
Chin-chin, etc.

AMALIA. *(To Paula.)*
What's the matter?

PAULA.
In the kitchen!

AMALIA.
What?

PAULA.
Rosa's brother, Santo. He's in the kitchen.

AMALIA. *(Beat.)* Open another bottle of wine. *(Amalia exits into the kitchen. Paula opens a bottle of wine and shakily pours around the table.)*

JUAN. Look out, you're splashing, Paula.

MADDALENA. *(Suddenly, startling everybody.)* To all the little white sheep coming home over the green fields of San Germano when the church bells call for the Angelus. *Salute! (She weeps and drinks the bicarbonate.)*

ALL except JUAN.
/ *(Respectfully.) Salute!*

LISE 2.
Baaaa ...

JUAN. / *(Overlapping.)* I'm not toasting any livestock at the dinner table! *Mamma,* please. Paula, sit down!

MADDALENA. This taste like feet. *(To Paula.)* You wanna kill me?

LISE 2. *Baaaa ...*

MADDALENA. Who is that?

JUAN. Your great-granddaughter Lise.

LISE 2. *Baaa ...*

MADDALENA. Why is she bleating?

LISE 2. *Baaa ...*

OTTO. Lise, stop.

MADDALENA. *(To Clara.)* I am a mountain girl. This Pampas here ... flat like pancake.

JUAN. There are huge, gigantic mountains here. What mulish ignorance! The Andes —

MADDALENA. Too big. Everything in America. Too big. No

heart. Even the cows too big. The Appennini not so big, *ma* they have heart. This country ... *(To Clara.)* They got the moon upside down! I'm dizzy alla time! Did you know I was *kidnappèd?*

LISE 2. *(Wailing.)* I don't like it here either!

LISE. So I ran away.

JUAN. Come on, *Mamma,* cheer up. Think of your favorite saint.

ELENA. The one with the breasts on a platter or the one with the eyes put out?

JUAN. Lena! Tell me what you want, *Mamma.* I never know what you want. Papa either.

MADDALENA. Do I know your father?

JUAN. Christ. *(Louder.)* What do you *want?*

MADDALENA. I want to be sixteen again in San Germano. *(Lise 2 wails.)*

JUAN. *(To the others.)* It rains nine months out of the year in San Germano. All I ever saw when I went there was mud.

AMALIA. *(Reentering, nervously.)* Why are you crying?

LISE 2. I don't know!

ELENA. I think Nonna and the succubus are getting a little sauced.

JUAN. *(To Alberto.)* Nothing makes women happy. *Nothing. (They eat. Amalia and Paula don't.)*

LISE 2. *(In the momentary silence.)* What's a foreskin? *(Everybody jumps. Rosa, entering with a steaming plate, turns around and exits.)*

AMALIA.	JUAN.	CLARA.	ELENA.
/ What?	My heart —	Oh, dear —	Good God ...

LISE. / *(Overriding.)* I knew that!

LISE 2. *(To Lise.)* Did not! *(To the others.)* What's a —

OTTO. We heard you the first time!

LISE 2. Sister Eulalia said New Year's Day is the day of the Circumcision of Jesus. That's when they cut your foreskin off, Aunt Paula says. Heidi Bleiman says it's in your forehead and they scalped him. *(General outrage.)*

PAULA. I never said *scalp!* The word *scalp* never crossed my lips!

AMALIA.	OTTO.	JUAN.	ALBERTO.
Otto!	It wasn't me!	I get pains up and down my left arm when I come to this house! Look! I can't feel my hand!	It's like having dinner in the Bermuda Triangle!

(All heads turn to Otto.)

OTTO. Oh — well — yes — uh — Amalia? *(All heads turn to*

44

Amalia.)

AMALIA. Thank you, Otto. Nobody scalped Jesus, darling.

LISE 2. Well they cut *something* off!

AMALIA. Oh, no dear. They just — they just — I have to see to the radishes. *(She exits.)*

OTTO. *(Shouting after her, a drowning man.)* What's to see?

LISE 2. *(Relentless.)* So what's a foreskin? *(Everybody hems and haws.)*

MADDALENA. *(Booming.)* It's useless flap on silly penis. You chop it off. *(The men choke, Paula sneezes.)*

LISE 2. *(Beat.)* What's a pe —

ALBERTO. / *(Rising.)* Oooh, well, look at the time, I have to pick someone up at the airport!

PAULA. / *(Idem and overlapping.)* My pills ...

CLARA. / *(Idem.)* Is that rain...?

OTTO. / *(Idem.)* I have to go move the car.

JUAN. / *(Idem.)* I'll just be in the bathroom shooting myself, in case anybody needs me.

ELENA. Sit down everybody! Just pretend she's not there. That's what I do. It's the only way.

LISE. I didn't find out till I was seventeen.

AMALIA. *(Reentering with a basket of bread. Very loud.)* And how was *Parsifal*, Aunt Clara?

CLARA. *(Chattering away.)* Terrifying! There was an *enormous* tenor who confused extreme youth with friskiness and recklessly skipped across the stage at the slightest provocation. Two of the Flower Maidens got run over and had to be carried out. The conductor was apoplectic and the brass section incapacitated. I left just as the French horns started to make tasteless sounds. *(Paula goes around the table drinking and pouring wine.)*

AMALIA. *(Sotto.)* Easy, Paula. Don't give Lise anymore, Papa.

JUAN. You want the child to grow up like a Quaker? *(To Lise.)* Quick, Bordeaux or Chianti? No looking at the bottle!

LISE 2. *(Takes a sip.)* Bordeaux!

JUAN. Good girl.

MADDALENA. *(Pushing her own glass away.)* Shouldn't drink the blood of Christ for pleasure.

JUAN. *Mamma, ti prego.* It is not the blood of Christ unless it's been consecrated!

ELENA. What should one do for pleasure, Nonna?

MADDALENA. Pray.

ALBERTO. *(Rising.)* If we're going to talk about God, I'm going home. Last time we talked about God here, someone let the air out of my tires. Somebody in *this* family! *(Elena pulls him back down.)*

OTTO. It took God billions of years to come up with man. It took man under five thousand to come up with Sophocles, Michelangelo, Shakespeare, Mozart ... What's there to talk about? *(The beginnings of half-hearted outrage from the half-hearted believers.)*

AMALIA. *(Briskly topping.)* Do you have a new play, Elena?

ELENA. *(Appalled.)* A new play?

AMALIA. You know, something new and exciting, to get back on the boards? Soon?

ELENA. What's the matter with you? Of course I don't have a new play. In fact not for quite some time now, which, if you took the *slightest* interest in my work, you might have noticed.

AMALIA. Well, bite my head off, why don't you. God.

ELENA. Don't you *ever* read the newspapers?

PAULA and AMALIA. The newspapers?

ELENA. You know, large squares of white paper with little black marks all over? *(To Alberto.)* This family!

CLARA. You've left the theatre, then?

ELENA. You now have to be a member of "the Party" to get a job in the National Theatre —

CLARA. Ah, yes ...

ELENA. — and since *all* professional theatres have been "nationalized," I can't work.

MADDALENA. Anarchists. Everywhere. Better check the bushes.

AMALIA. You never said ...

ELENA. You never asked ...

AMALIA. Couldn't you, I don't know, *lie* a little? / Where's the harm in that?

LISE. Indeed.

JUAN. / There are no anarchists here, *Mamma.*

MADDALENA. Sacco and Vanzetti!

JUAN. That was in *North* America.

MADDALENA. North, South, same mess.

ALBERTO. Excuse me, Sacco and Vanzetti were not —

MADDALENA. — *Italian,* I know! They was *Bolshevikkies!*

OTTO. *(Sotto voce.)* I tell you as a friend, Alberto. You don't want to pursue the subject of Sacco and Vanzetti around here. There was violence once. Cousins. A death.

CLARA. At our house it was Dreyfus. Went on for two generations.

AMALIA. First God, and then politics. Never fails.

ALBERTO.   What politics? You people believe in hereditary monarchy!

CLARA and MADDALENA.   What's wrong with that?

JUAN.   Easier to keep an eye on one imbecile than on forty crooks. *(Maddalena falls asleep, fork in hand.)*

ALBERTO.   If you don't get back on stage soon, they'll notice, Elena.

JUAN.   She doesn't need the stage. She needs a husband.

ELENA.   I'm not good in supporting roles.

JUAN.   Please, *carina.* For me. Enzo Rappetti married off all three of those buck-tooth heifers of his. He's been saying nobody want you. It's envy, you understand. I raised two beauties and he scared the whole neighborhood. Let me give you away to some good man.

AMALIA.   I should think Lena deserves more than a "good" man.

JUAN.   Who she waiting for, Toscanini?

ELENA.   Too short. And "a good man" is like *rosé wine* —

ELENA, LISE and AMALIA.   — a contradiction in terms … *(They laugh.)*

ALBERTO.   So, what, you're going to stay home and take up knitting?

ELENA.   I am not wearing any party badge and nobody tells me what I can and cannot play.

ALBERTO.   Then you'll have to leave the country.

ELENA.   Why should I leave the country? I am not political.

ALBERTO.   Don't be naive. You're not for them, you're against them.

LISE.   Why is this so / important all of a sudden…?

JUAN.   / *Ma, porca miseria!* Again with the politics!

AMALIA.   Well, let's not brood! It's Lise's birthday! Are you having fun, darling?

LISE 2.   *(Mouth full.)* No.

PAULA.   *(Cheerful.)* Does anybody know what a Nepalese sky burial is?

ALL.	LISE 2.
NO!	What is it?

PAULA.   They leave you on top of a mountain for the vultures to —

AMALIA.   No, no, no, Auntie Paula! Bad girl!

PAULA.   Of course, you're dead … *(Offstage voices. As before, Lise is involved with the Alberto-Elena argument and does not hear the other exchange.)*

OTTO.	ALBERTO.
Who's in the kitchen?	Argentine women have wanted the vote for

AMALIA.
Rosa, of course.

OTTO.
I thought I heard someone else.

AMALIA.
She's probably on the phone.

decades. Now that you
have it —
LISE.
1947! Unbelievable.

ELENA.
If they had *really* wanted
it they would have fought
for it. Very few did.
The rest of those cows
stayed home.

ELENA and LISE. / I hate this country! (/ *Otto crosses to the kitchen door and exits. Amalia rises.*)
AMALIA. / *(Overlap.)* Where are you going — wait —
ALBERTO. Then how do you expect to get rid of the son-of-a-bitch?
MADDALENA. *(Suddenly alert.)* Mussolini?
AMALIA. Mussolini's dead, Nonna.
MADDALENA. When?!
ELENA. Seven years ago!
MADDALENA. *(Beat.)* Did your grandfather have anything to do with it?
AMALIA. Grandpa died in 1930, Nonna.
MADDALENA. *Ah, certo.* The Welcher.
JUAN. Why, Italia, why? We give the world the Renaissance! How we come up with Benito Mussolini?
MADDALENA. Nothing but naked men, the Renaissance. Pitiful sight. *(Otto reenters and pulls Amalia aside.)*

ELENA.
I am *not* getting
dragged into a *mano a mano*
with that pond scum!
ALBERTO.
Look, I'm not talking about
setting fire to Congress —

OTTO.
(To Amalia.) Jesus, Malia, why
didn't you — That's who they're
looking for outside!
AMALIA.
What are we going to do?

JUAN.
I don't want my daughter
involved, Alberto!

OTTO.
I don't know …

AMALIA.
He can't stay here!

(Otto goes to window upstage.)
ELENA. *(To Alberto.)* This is my home. I refuse to become a tango

cliché and run off to die in Paris.

ALBERTO. How about the States?

ELENA. And do what there? Get a serious acting job from people who think Argentine women go about in puffy sleeves and hoop earrings, playing the castanets, balancing produce on their heads —

ELENA and LISE. — and have never heard of Ibsen? *(Offstage distant sirens.)*

JUAN. *(To Elena.)* You leave, you kill me. Remember that.

PAULA. But don't let it weigh heavy on your heart.

JUAN. Otto, what are you doing walking around back there? Sit down.

OTTO. No, I was looking for — Anyone for a little —

OTTO and LISE. — music? *(He opens the phonograph. Lise grabs the first record on hand and puts it on. It's Bastianini singing "Il Balen" from* Trovatore. *He turns the volume up, glances at the kitchen door and lights a cigarette.)*

CLARA and LISE. You smoke too much.

AMALIA. Who's singing?

OTTO. Bastianini. Great big lungs.

JUAN. Sereni's more musical.

OTTO. Too much *portamento,* Sereni.

EVERYBODY. *(Ad-lib. Immediate explosion.)* What do you mean too much *portamento?* / It's supposed to have *portamento!* / Well it's not what Verdi wanted! / You were there? / He scoops! / He does not! / When Hans Hotter sings Verdi — / Hans Hotter has no business singing Verdi, he should stick to *chalk!* / Titta Ruffo, now — / *Un porco fascista, Ruffo!* / He was not! / You knew him? / He's a bass! / Baritone! / Bass! / Baritone! / Bass! / Not a one who can hold a candle to Frank Sinatra / Cesare Siepi, now! / Wonderful thighs, Siepi. *(Etc.)*

JUAN. Listen to that voice! A young bull. *(One by one they all join in at the refrain with both Lises more or less in tune. Eventually they let fly and this music — the one constant in their lives — is their own.)*

ALL.

Ah, l'amor, l'amore ond'ardo,
Le favelli in mio favore,
Sperda il sole d'un suo sguardo
La tempesta del mio cor ... (Repeat.)

(The final cadenza is carried by Juan alone. The actor either mouths to Bastianini or, if possible, sings full out with him. Loud cheers and applause. A nearby dog howls. Rosa enters with the pasta.)

ROSA. Rutting seals make better noises. Make room. It's very hot. *(She places enormous steaming bowls on the table. Amalia begins to serve. The rest don't hear.)*

OTTO. / *(Sotto, to Rosa.)* What's he going to do?

ROSA. *(Idem.)* They have the others.

OTTO. *(Idem.)* Can you call someone? A friend?

ROSA. *(Idem.)* I'm afraid to. They listen on the line.

OTTO. *(Idem.)* Here?

ROSA. *(Idem.)* Everywhere. That's what he says. *(She continues serving with Amalia. Elena drinks a lot and eats very little. Otto goes back to windows.)*

MADDALENA. / The little girl is staring again.

AMALIA. She's your great-granddaughter.

MADDALENA. She's staring.

AMALIA. Lise, don't stare.

LISE 2. Why?

AMALIA. It's rude.

LISE. Why couldn't I look at my own family?

ELENA. I can't stay, I can't go. Nowhere. I'm nowhere.

ALBERTO. Why is it nobody loves this country?

PAULA. What we need is some champagne. *(She weaves to the cupboard where the champagne is on ice. Rosa exits.)*

ELENA. Steady there, Auntie.

PAULA. Considering that we're hurtling through space at this very moment dear, how steady can one expect to be? *(She starts to open a bottle. Otto is still hovering around the windows.)*

AMALIA. Otto …

CLARA. *(To Amalia.)* The rule at home also was: no religion or politics at the table.

ALBERTO. And look what happened to you.

LISE. Religion made people brood and politics was vulgar. I didn't vote till I was thirty.

OTTO. *(Returning to the table.)* Truth be told, Aunt Clara, we didn't spend much time on either.

CLARA. Indeed. *(To the others.)* We were a *mischling* family, you see; a Viennese concoction of Catholics and Jews intermarried for generations. Nobody kept track and nobody cared. We had an uncle who kept saying he should have been bar mitzvah'd in Notre Dame, kill two birds with one stone. They were forever careening between mass and the synagogue, atheists all, but unable to give it up. On purely *aesthetic* grounds, you understand. Come Rosh Hashanah, they would suddenly appear in a pack, lurching down the street towards temple wildly intent on "preserving tradition." It seldom mattered *which* tradition and they *always* got the dates wrong. "Who are those people?" would ask poor Rabbi Rosenthal. "Oh God, it's the Bergs, again," would say Rabbi Herzler. "The Bergs?" would say Rabbi Rosenthal, "Aren't they Catholics"? "Not this week," would moan Rabbi Herzler. And they would both run away. Mind you, dear Father Reinhardt didn't want them either because they were disorderly when mass was not well sung and rowdy when it was. No sense of occasion at all. And on top of everything else they were *all* Socialists, so they were completely unpresentable.

OTTO. How could Uncle Freddy be a Socialist, he was a bank president! *(To the others.)* It's a family delusion.

CLARA. He had a deep sense of *noblesse oblige!* We had ideals, no matter what our station in life. People who wanted to *count* for something had ideals!

ALBERTO. Somewhere along the line the politics has to go along with the ideals, or it's all for nothing, Mrs. Stepaneck.

CLARA. Oh, but it did! Why, Freddy's most prized possession was a signed photo of FDR which he kept on his desk.

JUAN. *(Gravely.)* A sainted man, rest in peace.

PAULA. So good to the little people.

LISE. To this day I can't think of FDR except surrounded by the seven dwarves. *(Police sirens stop just under the windows. Car doors opening and slamming shut. Alberto goes to the window again followed by Elena.)*

ELENA. Is that a — a roundup of some kind?

JUAN. Sit down, everybody! We're going to toast my granddaughter and have some cake.

ROSA. *(Entering.)* Salad first. I didn't make it for nothing. *(Doorbell.)*

ELENA. I'll get it.

OTTO. No, wait!

ELENA. It's all right. *(She exits. / Paula pours champagne for all, sometimes into their plates. Otto looks at Rosa who shakes her head "no.")*

OTTO. / *(Sotto.)* The fire door.

ROSA. *(Idem.)* There's people in the alley.

OTTO. *(Idem.)* Try the service door on the other side. *(Rosa puts the salad down and exits, followed by Otto. Henri enters with Elena. He's in full gala uniform for the first time. He looks dazzling.)*

AMALIA. *(Frozen.)* — Just in time for a little champers!

LISE 2. Uncle H! You look like a — a *hero!*

51

HENRI. For your birthday, princess. *(She runs to him.)*
AMALIA. Don't! You've dirty hands, darling. *(He picks her up and gives her a gift-wrapped book. She opens it.)*
OTTO. *(Reenters. Stops.)* What a nice surprise. Please join us. Sit down, Lise.
LISE 2. *Alice's Adventures in Wonderland* ... *(With great distaste.)* Is this about *girls?*
HENRI. No, it's about rabbits.
AMALIA. *(Nervously.)* We thought you'd be working late, so we didn't — Where's Angelica?
HENRI. *(Beat.)* At her parents', in the country.
JUAN. A glass of claret, Henri?
HENRI. Thank you, yes. *(To Clara.)* A pleasure to see you again, Mrs. Stepaneck.
CLARA. *(High Viennese ice.)* The pleasure is mine.
AMALIA. You remember Henri Fontannes, Nonna.
MADDALENA. No.
HENRI. *(Charming.)* Ah, but I remember *you,* Mrs. Guarneri. Where have you been keeping yourself, Elena? Your public misses you.
ELENA. I've been vacationing at Papa's.
HENRI. You're looking well.
ELENA. Am I? *(She holds his look a fraction of a second.)* Good for me.
LISE. What was that? *(To Amalia.)* Did you notice that?
AMALIA. Notice what ...
LISE. That — between the two of them ... Did they — *(To Lise 2, who's been reading her book.)* Pay attention!
LISE 2. To what?
HENRI. And how's the newspaper business, Alberto?
ALBERTO. Thriving. Like the broadcasting business. *(Uncomfortable pause. Amalia crosses to the kitchen door.)*
AMALIA. Rosa, would you bring another plate? *(Rosa appears at the door.)*
HENRI. Oh, no, please don't bother. Thanks. *(Beat.)* Good evening, Rosa.
ROSA. Evening, sir. *(She exits.)*
AMALIA. A little *bouillon* at least? I bet you haven't had anything all day.
HENRI. Not hungry. It smells delicious, though. *(They eat. Silence.)*
PAULA. *(Suddenly, to Henri, in a tiny voice.)* They say tulip bulbs, if they're not replanted every year, burrow deeper and deeper into the ground until they disappear altogether. Do you suppose they

52

pop up in Australia? *(A bewildered silence.)* I need a teensy-weensy little more champagne, please. *(She goes to pour, Juan takes the bottle away from her.)*

HENRI. You like gardening, Paula?

PAULA. Loathe it. *(Hiccough. Silence.)*

MADDALENA. *(Abruptly, to Henri.)* Did you know I was *kidnappèd?*

HENRI. Were you?

AMALIA. *(To Henri.)* Do *not* encourage that line of conversation.

PAULA. I would pay someone. A *lot of money* ... *(More sirens outside.)*

LISE. *(Annoyed.)* What *is* / that?

MADDALENA. *(Overlap.)* / What's all the racket?

PAULA. Fires. I expect. So cold.

MADDALENA. *(Fateful.)* Ambulance. *(To Paula.)* Is for you.

ALBERTO. Those are police sirens.

JUAN. How nice to be here together! *Salute! (/ Rosa enters and continues serving salad around the table, fresh bread, refilling water glasses, etc.)*

LISE 2. / *(Reading.)* " ... what would become of me? They're dreadfully fond of beheading people here: the great wonder is — *(Lise has gone to the window and looks out.)*

LISE 2 and LISE. " — that there's anyone left alive!" *(Rosa exits.)*

LISE 2. This is great, Uncle H!

CLARA. Time for more presents, Liesl! *(She takes a long thin black velvet box from her handbag and gives it to Lise 2, who opens it. It's a white lace fan.)* For later.

LISE 2. Everything's for "later."

LISE. Nothing was ever for "now" ...

CLARA. It belonged to my mother.

OTTO. The Brahms fan!

CLARA. When she was very young, Mother went to hear Brahms play at somebody's house. As he was leaving she asked him to sign her fan, and so he wrote the opening bars to "The Blue Danube Waltz" on it and under them, "Unfortunately not by Johannes Brahms." *(To Lise 2.)* A little bit of the Vienna you'll never know because the boots came in. *(They pass the fan around.)*

ALBERTO. The boots seldom come in uninvited. Somebody said that. Do you know who, Otto?

OTTO. No. *(Lise 2 weeps.)*

AMALIA. What's the matter now?

53

LISE 2. *(She wails.)* It makes me *saaaad!*

AMALIA. It's beautiful, Clara. Let me put it away, Lise.

LISE 2. I don't want to.

AMALIA. Well, don't cry anymore then.

LISE 2. *(Wailing louder.)* I like to cry!

AMALIA. It's the wine. You see, Papa?

ELENA. To my niece, the Tiny Tippler. *Salut.*

AMALIA. Why don't we put away the pretty fan and save it for your coming-out party?

LISE 2. *(Howling.)* That's not for years! *(Fireworks start outside and glow behind the window panes.)*

HENRI. Look! Fireworks!

OTTO. Just for you.

LISE 2. *(Sniffling.)* For me?

AMALIA. Otto, really. Don't use your sleeve, dear. They're for the feast of St. John.

HENRI. Who just happens to share your birthday. *(Henri puts a tango — "Por Una Cabeza" — on the phonograph. Crossing to Lise 2.)* Mademoiselle?

LISE. No, no, no. I danced with Papi. Didn't I? This is all *wrong!* *(Lights change. Henri and Lise 2 dance a tango around the table, Lise 2 whipping her braids about, flashing toothless smiles right and left, while fireworks explode in the night outside. Everybody applauds except Otto. Sounds like pistol shots are heard among the fireworks.)*

CLARA. *(Half rising.)* What's that?

MADDALENA. / *(Matter-of-fact.)* Gunshots.

AMALIA. *(Overlap.)* / Roman candles. They've started the bonfires.

MADDALENA and LISE. / *(Louder.)* Gunshots.

CLARA. / Ah, bonfires, yes! In Europe too! It's Midsummer Night there, you know.

ALBERTO. *(Eyes on the window.)* Walpurgisnacht. *(Otto stops the music. Lights restore.)*

OTTO. That's enough, Lise.

LISE 2. What? Why?

OTTO. Your poor Uncle H has been working all day. A little more wine, Henri?

HENRI. *(Stopped short.)* Thanks. *(He sits. Paula reaches for wine which is swiftly removed from her grasp. Her hand lands in the salad bowl.)*

PAULA. Ooop-sie … *(Hiccough.)* … Sorry … *(She staggers to the sideboard and swats at a few bottles before grabbing the port.)* Here we are! *Oporto!* All the way from Lisbon.

MADDALENA. That pig Franco still live there? *(/ General discomfort. Paula pours an enormous tumbler of port and places it before Henri. Amalia removes it immediately and puts down a glass of Bordeaux.)*

ALBERTO. / Madrid, Nonna.

LISE 2. Who's Pig Franco?

OTTO.   JUAN.
Nobody.   Never mind.

AMALIA. We don't say "Franco" at the table, darling.

ELENA. We're ready for that cake now, Rosa! *(Rosa puts her head in.)*

ROSA. Well, I'm not! *(She disappears.)*

ELENA. Fine.

JUAN. *(To Henri.)* I'm having some wonderful venison steaks sent —

LISE 2. YOU'RE GONNA EAT BAMBI?!

ELENA. No dear, Bambi's *mother* ...

LISE 2. WHAT?!

HENRI. *(Quickly.)* Any news from Italy, Mrs. Guarneri?

MADDALENA. We got rid of that pig Mussolini. *(Paula drinks from the bottle on the sideboard. Amalia takes it away from her. Food is pushed around the plates. Nobody eats.)*

JUAN. / Mamma!

ELENA. / *(Overlap, to Lise 2.)* Speaking of *Walpurgisnacht* ... *(She pulls out a tall broom with a large red bow from behind a door, or the window drapes.)* Till you're old enough to drive, darling. Happy birthday. *(General laughter. Lise 2 glowers.)*

AMALIA. Oh, she's just a little girl ...

ELENA. So was Lady Macbeth once.

MADDALENA. *(Suddenly, to Henri.)* You in the government?

HENRI. Yes, Mrs. Guarneri.

MADDALENA. None of my business because I'm not from around here but ... time to get rid of this pig Perón, no? What you think? *(Forks drop on plates. Pause.)*

HENRI. *(Winking at Otto.)* I'll keep that in mind, Mrs. Guarneri.

PAULA. *(Rising, frantic.)* She's having one of her spells!

MADDALENA. Who is ...

ELENA. *(Overlap.)* Time for Nonna's nap! *(The women surround her at once and start pulling her away from the table.)*

JUAN. *(To Henri.)* A fixation.

AMALIA. *(Idem.)* She's ninety-seven.

CLARA. *(Idem, babbling inanely.)* A grief-stricken woman ... the

Atlantic crossing, you know …

PAULA. *(Idem.)* All last night she thought her bedspread was the Shroud of Turin.

MADDALENA. *(As she's being carted off, fork in hand, napkin still around her neck.)* What's going on? What's going on?

JUAN. *(To Henri.)* My poor father tried to make her happy, but —

MADDALENA. *(On her way out.)* Not hard enough!

ELENA. *(Following.)* It's a picnic with the Borgias.

MADDALENA. *(Offstage.)* I heard that!

ELENA. *(At the door.)* Of course you did!

AMALIA. *(Exiting.)* You want to lie down a little, Nonna.

MADDALENA. *(Offstage.)* No, I don't!

PAULA. *(Offstage.)* YES YOU DO, MOTHER!

LISE 2. *(Offstage. Helpful.)* I'll read to you from *Dracula*, Nonna.

MADDALENA. *(Offstage.)* I not stay alone with the Bad Seed! Take her away! Take her away!

AMALIA. *(Offstage.)* Go back to the table, Lise.

LISE 2. *(Offstage.)* Hell. *(She reenters with Clara. Suspicious.)* What's "the Bad Seed"?

ALBERTO. Does this family ever talk about, you know, the weather?

ELENA. *(Reentering.)* Only when we mean something else.

HENRI. *(Politely.)* Why did you leave Vienna, Mrs. Stepaneck?

ELENA. *(Can't help herself.)* On holiday?

HENRI. No, I mean, you're not Jewish …

CLARA. Oh, but I am. In 1941 I married a Jew. I converted.

ALBERTO. Who converts to Judaism in the middle of World War II?

OTTO. People in my family.

LISE. Oh! There was insanity on *both* sides!

CLARA. And my brother was arrested during one of the university purges. *(Beat.)* He taught the Romantics. Who would have thought they were a problem?

ALBERTO. Romantics are always a problem, Mrs. Stepaneck. We lose them right and left these days. It's an epidemic.

JUAN. Alberto …

HENRI. That's all right. Alberto and I go back a long way.

ALBERTO. That's … ancient history.

HENRI. You make us sound like a couple of decrepit old men!

ALBERTO. Yes, I imagine it's hard to feel grown-up in fancy dress.

HENRI. *(Beat.)* Ridiculous, isn't it? *(Unbuttoning his collar.)* And

56

hot. Had to attend a function. *(To the others.)* You won't believe this but "old" Alberto here used to be a lot of fun in school.
ALBERTO. Yes, well ...
HENRI. The physics lab blow-up ... The whoopee-cushions in second-year Latin ... The goat in the women's gym ...
CLARA. A goat — ?
HENRI. *His* idea.
ALBERTO. My idea, his goat.
CLARA. And the ladies?
ALBERTO. A howling mob with hockey sticks and scary shoes. We had to hide out at his parents' for a week. Then we were suspended. *(General laughter.)*
HENRI. We were young ...
ALBERTO. We were *very* young ... *(Rosa and Amalia enter with a huge ornate chocolate cake blazing with candles. General jubilation.)*
AMALIA. OK, make a wish and blow. *(Lise 2 does. Applause.)*
JUAN. *(Rising.)* As the proud grandfather, I reserve the right to make the first toast. *(All ad-lib agreement.)* To my granddaughter Lise, on her birthday: music, sun, wine and happiness all the days of her life. *(Aside.)* And a better disposition. *(To Lise.)* We won't be so young when we meet again. *(To Otto.)* Old Viennese toast. *Salute!*
ALL. *(Overlapping.)* Chin-chin / *Salute!* / *Prosit!* *(They gather around the cake. Juan leads them in a stanza of "Brindisi" from* Traviata. *Paula, reentering, joins them loudly. They're all a little drunk.)*

> Godiamo, godiamo, la tazza e il cantico
> La notte abbella e il riso;
> In questo, in questo paradiso
> Ne scopra il nuovo di.

HENRI. *(Toasting her with his glass of wine.)* The world, princess. *(They suddenly notice Henri, isolated at the end of the table.)*
AMALIA. Oh Lord, we gave you no champagne!
HENRI. Thank you, I only dropped by for a moment. My desk is piled to the ceiling with work. Happy birthday, baby. *(He kisses Lise 2 on top of her head. She throws her arms around him and kisses him on the cheek. A rare display of affection.)*
LISE 2. *(Disappointed.)* Where are you going?
HENRI. Who's my best buddy?
LISE 2 and LISE. Me!
HENRI. Good night, all. Don't get up, please. Ladies.
AMALIA. Good night. Otto? I have to get the coffee. *(Otto walks*

Henri out. Amalia exits into the kitchen. The table is silent. Juan whistles "Di quell'amor" from La Traviata.)

HENRI. *(Aside with Otto.)* There seems to be a — some sort of problem outside. Don't open the door. To *anyone.*

OTTO. What's going on?

HENRI. Nothing to worry about. But make sure everybody stays put. For a while.

OTTO. What — are *you* doing out there, tonight?

HENRI. *(Beat.)* Looking after you.

OTTO. Please — don't.

HENRI. I got a phone call telling me there was something — *amiss* in my neck of the woods.

OTTO. Really? Well, *we're* fine. As you can see. No need to —

HENRI. But I want to. Remember: stay put.

OTTO. I'll tell Amalia. *(Henri exits. Amalia comes back with coffee pot and serves coffee.)*

ELENA. Sugar ... *(Unnoticed, she exits into the kitchen. Paula jumps up and follows. Lise 2, also unnoticed, goes around the table emptying wine glasses into her person.)*

ALBERTO. *(Pacing.)* Awfully chummy with the general, weren't we?

JUAN. Son, I'd make friends with the devil were he to move in next door to my daughter.

ALBERTO. No, I mean, how do I end up in college-buddy, hail-fellow-well-met chit-chat with the guy —

JUAN. What's the problem here? We all *like* the man ...

ALBERTO. *That's* the problem, don't you see?

OTTO. Is there another course of action you'd like to suggest?

ALBERTO. He goes in and out of here like — The man thinks this is — what, his *family* for God's sake! And we're still in school? What's that all about?

OTTO. He's trying very hard to stay within the marking posts, or he'll go all adrift. Like us.

LISE. Adrift? / We were not *adrift* ...

ALBERTO. / Yes, well. You don't get points for trying. As the catastrophe that was Europe has shown.

OTTO. You don't know. You weren't there.

ALBERTO. History doesn't have to repeat itself. It isn't an unstoppable machine.

OTTO. What do you know? You know nothing here in America!

AMALIA. *(Taking over.)* I'm sorry, Alberto. We're all out of sorts lately. I promise you a better *soirée* very soon.

ALBERTO. This house. Lines get crossed here. Before you know it you can't tell where you are anymore. I need air. Thank you for dinner. Good night. *(He kisses her on the cheek.)*
OTTO. He said not to go out there.
ALBERTO. I am not going to sit here wallowing in Old World *schmaltz* while the country's going to hell. Europe was my *parents'* home, not mine. Now if you'll excuse me, I have a newspaper to run. *(He exits.)*
JUAN. *(Shouting after him.)* Dead people don't run anything! Damn! *(Lise 2 has fallen asleep. Elena enters from the kitchen followed by Paula.)*
PAULA. / I'm sorry, Amalia — she got past me and —
ELENA. / *(Overlapping, to Otto and Amalia.)* Are you out of your minds? Jesus Christ, get rid of him!
OTTO. Surely there's something we can do. There *must* be —
ELENA, JUAN and LISE. What ... What are you talking about? What...?
OTTO. — something — think — Let me *think* for a moment —
ELENA. Think? What's to *think?*
JUAN. What the hell's going on?
OTTO. Rosa's brother Santo. The one in trouble with the police. He's here.
JUAN. Where ...
ELENA. In the kitchen, for God's sake! All evening!
LISE. Who is this person?
AMALIA. He came to see his sister.

JUAN.	CLARA.	LISE.
Madonna Santa!	*Gott in Himmel ...*	What's this all about?

OTTO. *(To Juan, abruptly.)* Take him to the country with you.
JUAN. *To my house?*
OTTO. Can't you hide him in the vineyards, the stables, the barn, I don't know, somewhere?
JUAN. Are you crazy?
OTTO. One more field hand. Who would know?
JUAN. ... For how long?
OTTO. I don't know.
AMALIA. What are you doing, Otto?
JUAN. How do we get him there?
AMALIA. Papa!
OTTO. In the back of your car.
ELENA. / There are road checks!

59

JUAN. / This cloak-and-dagger stuff, Otto — Please, I'm too old. I can't —

PAULA. / Oh, no, no, no …

LISE. / When did this happen? This never happened …

OTTO. / *(To Elena.)* You sit in back and throw your fur coat over him. They won't search your car.

ELENA. What, you think the friendly guys in the helmets are going to ask for my autograph and say, "We loved you in *Mary Stuart*, Miss Guarneri! Sorry we have to bludgeon you and throw your body in a ditch"?

AMALIA. Papa!

OTTO. It's a two-hour drive on country roads and it's the middle of the night. You won't be stopped.

AMALIA. NO!

JUAN. Why? Tell me why we must do this? This — foolish thing? It's none of our business! Why?

ELENA. *(Beat.)* Let's. *(She downs another glass of wine.)*

AMALIA. You can't!

ELENA. *(Downing another glass of wine.)* Quickly. Or I'll change my mind.

OTTO. Get the car around the back, Juan.

AMALIA. Don't be ridiculous! What —

ELENA. Watch out for the doorman.

JUAN. I'm parked out in front. He's going to wonder why I'm driving around in circles like the village idiot.

CLARA. I'll go downstairs and make him get me a taxi around the corner. It'll take him a while.

OTTO. Do you think you could?

AMALIA. / My God. What's *wrong* with everybody?

CLARA. / *(Overlap.)* Why couldn't I? And Paula's going to help me.

PAULA. Oh … I don't know …

ELENA. *(A touch over the top.)* Oh, for once in your life, let yourself go! *(Beat, alarmed.)*

LISE. *(Outraged.)* That's from *Uncle Vanya*!

ELENA. Chekhov knew everything.

CLARA. *(To Paula.)* You chatter to him in one ear and I in the other. He won't know which way is front. Come along, dear.

PAULA. Please, no, don't ask me. I couldn't. I'm sorry. No nerve … never did have … *(She exits into the house.)*

JUAN. *(Putting on his hat and coat.)* I'll drive around after I got him and pick you up. What am I saying…!

AMALIA. Papa, please. Everybody's had too much to drink — the children, Nonna —

LISE. / No, no, no. Wait a second — What's happening here? My birthday — my party — It's all wrong ...

OTTO. / Drive up to the service door. I'll check the side street and bring him down to you.

ELENA. Wait. What about *him?*

OTTO. Who?

ELENA. Next door. What if he hears us?

AMALIA. / Stop it!

OTTO. / Hear what? People going home after a party? He's heard us a thousand times.

JUAN. All right. / Let's go. *Santo Dio.*

ELENA. / God forgive me, but this is thrilling.

AMALIA. *(Taking over.) THERE ARE TWO SMALL CHILDREN HERE! (Everybody stops. Rosa enters. Pause.)*

ROSA. He's gone. He wanted you to know, so you won't worry.

JUAN. He's ... gone?

ELENA. But —

OTTO. He's gone ...

ROSA. He wouldn't have come but that he was so hungry. He didn't mean to bring trouble. *(Motions towards the dinner table.)* Shall I pick up now?

AMALIA. No ... no, thank you, Rosa. I — I'm —

ROSA. He scared me too. *(Rosa exits. Pause.)*

OTTO. Trouble ... no, we could have —

AMALIA. As it turns out we couldn't.

OTTO. He went back out there.

JUAN. *(His coat still on, by the door.)* It's out of our hands, Otto.

OTTO. What a relief, eh?

AMALIA. Don't.

OTTO. We talked too much. All evening we talked. About opera.

LISE. But we *always* did that.

OTTO. Of course we can do that, snug and cozy as we are. Because we're *protected.* We have special protection.

AMALIA. Stop it.

OTTO. We are being "looked after," did you know, Juan?

JUAN. We tried.

OTTO. We did? Hard? *Very* hard? Or just a little hard? Or —

JUAN. Otto, you can't — This is not your problem. You have a family to think about.

61

OTTO. Our very own little group, eh? A *tiny* little knot, in fact. How tight do you think we can make it before we choke to death?

LISE. This is not how I remember my birthday.

ELENA. Alberto's right. I should leave the country.

JUAN. Oh, let's *not* turn this into a tragedy now.

OTTO. Oh, no. No tragedy at all. For us.

JUAN. Well, what's the use — *(Beat.)* Damn!

LISE. It wasn't like this! *(To Lise 2.)* Was it? *(She notices Lise 2 fast asleep, head on the table. To Lise 2.)* Oh, come on! *(She quickly puts on a old, scratchy record of Tauber singing "Wien du Stadt meiner Traüme." Otto lights a cigarette.)*

AMALIA. I'll take her. *(She picks Lise 2 up and starts to walk out of the room.)*

LISE 2. *(Half-asleep.)* What's going on? What'd I miss?

LISE. *BLOODY EVERYTHING!*

AMALIA. Nothing important, dear. Shhhh. Let's put you in bed.

LISE 2. Who's in the kitchen?

AMALIA.	OTTO.
Nobody.	A hero.
LISE 2.	LISE.
(Wide awake.) What?!	Nobody ever told me …

AMALIA. Bed. *(They exit.)*

LISE 2. *(Offstage.)* Hell.

ELENA. *(Still by the window, lighting cigarette.)* One often stands in grave danger of not knowing who one *is* … *(Elena kisses her father and absently waves good night to the rest. She exits.)*

OTTO. Oh, I think we know *exactly* who we are. Now.

JUAN. *(Shouting after her.)* You're my beautiful daughter Elena Guarneri, that's who you are! These are things not for women to worry about! *(Lise 2 reappears with her headless doll.)*

LISE 2. How come my guardian angel never appears to me?

JUAN. *(Taking his coat off.)* He's applying for another job.

LISE 2. Grandfathers are supposed to be friendly. *(She exits.)*

LISE. *(To Otto.)* Listen … *(From the phonograph, Tauber sings.)*

TAUBER.
> Wien, Wien, nur du allein,
> sollst stets die Stadt meiner Traüme sein …

CLARA. Exiles from our youth, is what we are. Oh, we're such — trivial people … *(Paula wanders into the room.)*

PAULA. *(Matter-of-fact.)* She doesn't like women, my mother. And women who don't like women dislike their daughters most of

all. *(Offstage a baby cries.)*
AMALIA. *(Offstage.)* I'll see to him.
PAULA. *(To no one.)* I should have left in the night. Gone off.
Danced. I should have danced ...
TAUBER.

> Dort wo die alten Haüser stehn,
> dort wo die lieblichen Mädchen geh'n ...

AMALIA. *(Offstage.)* Did you bolt the back door, Rosa?
ROSA. *(Offstage.)* Not yet.
JUAN. Beautiful voice, Tauber. A little Germanic, but —
OTTO and LISE. Viennese.
ROSA. *(Offstage.)* I have to put the milk bottles out.
JUAN. What?
OTTO. *Viennese.* Entirely different thing.
JUAN. Yes. Beautiful.
AMALIA. *(Offstage.)* And close all the shutters.
PAULA. *(Digging into her purse.)* Where are my pills ...
JUAN. *(Lighting a cigar.)* This we have. And Bjørling and the
Greek girl, what's-her-name ... This they can't take away. This they
can't touch.
AMALIA. *(Crossing upstage.)* It stinks of nostalgia in here. *(Exits.)*
CLARA. What would we do without music?
OTTO. I don't know. *(Paula pours herself a glass of water and takes
some pills.)*
LISE. Where do you get those ...
PAULA. Your mother ... *(She waltzes slowly and unsteadily around
the room. Lise turns the music up. Otto and Juan hum along at the
table and smoke. Through the windows, if possible, we see Rosa in the
fire escape looking down, her face lit by the revolving red lights of the
police cars.)* The bloom of a cloud, the crest of a wave ... I could
have flown. *(Hiccough. In the distance, the siren of a police car driving away. Paula stumbles over a chair and it crashes to the ground.)*
TAUBER.

> Dort wo ich glücklich und selig bin,
> ist Wien, ist Wien, mein Wien ...

(Police sirens receding in the distance.)

End of Act Two

63

ACT THREE

Scene 1

At house lights, the "Flower Duet" from Madama Butterfly. *Evening, a month later. Elena reads a newspaper, lounging on the sofa. Clara, crocheting a delicate piece, and Maddalena, scowling at the universe, sit together on a settee. Paula watches the rain through the window. Lise 2 colors in a book on the rug. Amalia enters with a tea tray followed by Rosa who places a sachertorte on the tea table and exits.*

AMALIA. Here we are.
MADDALENA. Who drink tea? The sick and the English!
AMALIA. Here's your coffee, Nonna. Careful, it's hot.
CLARA. So terribly cold outside. In Europe nobody ever thinks of South America being cold.
AMALIA. They never think far enough South.
PAULA. *(At window.)* ... nothing to remember ...
CLARA. Ah, yes, the warm South, the cold North ... ignorance ...
ELENA. Best lover I ever had was a Swede ...
AMALIA. Lise dear, there's no need to hang on your auntie's *every* word.
PAULA. *(To Elena.)* They say Alsatians, actually ...
ELENA. *(To Amalia.)* At her age I was already in the initial stages of my first *grande passion*: Rodolfo Valentino in *The Sheik*.
LISE 2. What's a *grande passion*?
LISE. A nervous disorder.
MADDALENA. *(To Lise.)* Two husbands ... *Bigamist!*
LISE. Christ.
AMALIA. Milk and sugar, Clara?
CLARA. Lemon, please.
AMALIA. Paula?
PAULA. Hemlock.
AMALIA. Heaven's sake ...

CLARA. Paris is suffocating right now ...

AMALIA. Elena?

ELENA. *(Reading the paper.)* Rum.

AMALIA. In your tea?

ELENA. Yes.

CLARA. My father always put rum in his tea.

AMALIA. I don't know if we have any. *(She crosses to cabinet. During the following speech we may see Rosa out in the fire escape, looking out in the rain, and subsequently a glimpse of a "woman in white:" Leila's ghost.)*

LISE. It was one of those dull, uneventful evenings I loathed as a child, when my mother and the others flocked around Nonna, lithe and slim-hipped, on high heels and seamed stockings like herons picking their careful way around a squawking old crow. Sounds: the incessant clinking of bone china, snapping of cigarette lighters, rustling of silk, and above all, the senseless *chatter* which never got louder than the cooing of doves at nightfall but seemed to pull all the air out of the room. I found women unendurable and secretly longed for the day I would escape so as not to become like them or like Cousin Leila, whose lissome ghost I would catch out of the corner of my eye weaving a noiseless path among the others, stirring spoonfuls of poison into a petal-thin, silver-rimmed porcelain cup.

CLARA. *(Checking her watch.)* Otto not home yet?

AMALIA. No. *(Elena looks up. Amalia finds a bottle of rum and pours some in Elena's tea.)* Rosa makes the most wonderful sachertorte, Clara. Paula, would you cut? You do it best. I always manage to crush it.

PAULA. It's all in the wrist. You must keep a flexible wrist, as for the piano, and use a chilled, long, round-tipped knife. *(Paula cuts the cake with exquisite care.)*

CLARA. It's very difficult to cut cake.

PAULA. Oh, Argentina's full of superfluous women my age with migraines and a hysterical bent who cut cake to perfection. *(No transition.)* Where do you suppose that boy is? Santo?

CLARA and AMALIA. It's been a month. Let's not ...

ELENA. Are we going to be morbid?

AMALIA. It's the rain. How was the Bonino wedding?

ELENA. Weeeelll ... we had an itsy-bitsy *contretemps.* You tell it, Auntie Paula.

PAULA. They're very spiteful people, *very* spiteful. *All* I said —

ELENA. She congratulated the groom and extended her condolences to the bride. Loudly.

AMALIA. Oh, Paula. She did that at the Serna wedding too. They haven't spoken to us since.

PAULA. I watched those bright young women grow up. They had such plans! And then: death by marriage.

AMALIA. Bright young girls also want families. More tea, Clara?

PAULA. Breeding is not a *purpose* dear, it's biology. A baboon can reproduce. Other than exhibiting its backside, it has no other occupation. Look what happened to your Aunt Aida after nine children.

LISE 2. She went around showing people her backside?

AMALIA. She most certainly did not!

LISE. Was she the bridge-jumper?

PAULA. No, that was Vittoria.

MADDALENA. My sister Immacolata 'ave seventeen children.

PAULA. Dead at forty-five.

AMALIA. A little cake, Nonna?

MADDALENA. Cake's baby food.

LISE 2. What happened to Aunt Aida?

AMALIA. Drink your cocoa.

MADDALENA. And my cousin Annunziata 'ave ten and a half.

CLARA. *Half a child?*

MADDALENA. An idiot.

CLARA. I'm *so* sorry.

MADDALENA. Sorry, nothing. *Un porco fascista!* She have to shoot 'im.

CLARA. *(Choking on her tea.)* Oh my God!

AMALIA.	ELENA.	PAULA.
I assure you there's been no murder in this family! Give her some water. Or not …	Put your arms up! Did you get it on your dress?	Goodness, Nonna! The woman will say anything!

(They tend to Clara. Maddalena, oblivious, drinks her coffee and hums "Cuore 'ngrato.")

LISE 2 and LISE. What happened to Aunt Aida, Paula?

PAULA. *(Mouthed, no voice.)* I'll tell you later.

AMALIA. I want to hear all about the wedding.

MADDALENA. Weddings. Ha! *(Balefully to Clara.)* I have one of those. "Marry a boy from San Germano," *Mamma* say. But no! The Welcher come over the mountain with flowers and he fill my head with talk of boats and the high seas. "Across the sea is beautiful" he

66

say. How he know? He never been anywhere. But: I believe because he bring white lilac in the afternoon. You smell lilac, you can't think, then you end up on the other side of the world. Terrible things, flowers. *(Darkly.)* Men who bring you flowers have *plans*. *(To Lise 2.) You* don't got nothing to worry about. *(She makes the sign of the "malocchio." They scowl at each other.)* So now I'm here … with the goddamn Black Shirts.

AMALIA. That was Mussolini, dear.

MADDALENA. He had the Brown Shirts.

CLARA. No, that was Hitler.

MADDALENA. Who does Perón have?

ELENA. The No-Shirts.

MADDALENA. *(Beat.)* I can't keep up.

AMALIA. How did the groom's party look?

PAULA. *(Darkly.)* Like a posse.

AMALIA. And the bridesmaids?

ELENA. You couldn't see for the diamonds.

AMALIA. Terribly fond of beads, those girls.

CLARA. I wouldn't be seen *poached* in diamonds. Diamonds are for chippies.

ELENA. *(Reading the newspaper.)* Nothing but progress reports on the dismal woman's illness. *(Otto enters from the outside.)*

CLARA. Hello, dear.

OTTO. Hello, Aunt Clara. Ladies. Hello, monkey.

LISE 2. What's a chippy?

OTTO. *(To Amalia.)* Why can't she *ever* ask about geography, math, finger painting?

AMALIA. "It is foolish to be surprised when a fig tree produces figs."

LISE 2. *(Outraged.)* I don't finger paint!

AMALIA. You're dripping. *(He takes his raincoat off and hangs it in the hallway.)*

ELENA. *(Casually.)* Where have you been?

OTTO. Walking.

CLARA. Without an umbrella?

OTTO. I had one. Don't know what happened to it.

LISE 2. How come *I* don't get to walk around outs —

OTTO. Give it a rest, Lise.

LISE 2. Fine.

AMALIA. Tea?

OTTO. Any coffee?

AMALIA. In the kitchen. *(Going to the door.)* Rosa!

OTTO. Don't.

AMALIA. It'll only take a sec —

OTTO. Don't! Tea is fine. What have you ladies been doing?

AMALIA. *(Pouring tea.)* Oh, chatting about the weather and cake and wedding dresses.

OTTO. How very nice. You've no idea.

AMALIA. What's it like out?

OTTO. *(Lighting a cigarette.)* Cold. Windy. Wet. Dark. A mess. *(Beat.)* You haven't heard?

AMALIA. What?

OTTO. She's dead.

ELENA and CLARA. What? The woman?

OTTO. She died. Turn the radio on. *(Elena turns on the large Zenith radio. Mid-broadcast. It continues under the scene until Amalia turns the radio off.)*

RADIO. *(V.O.)* ... *at eight twenty-five tonight, the spiritual leader of the nation, Eva Perón passed into immortality. The entire nation mourns the loss of a hero.*

LISE 2. *(Suddenly alert.)* "Hero"? *(Drum rolls. Chopin's "Funeral March.")*

ELENA. *(Singing.)* Ding dong...!

AMALIA. Lena, she's dead.

ELENA. We're all going to die. It doesn't give anybody a moral advantage. *(Paula starts laughing softly.)*

MADDALENA. Who's dead?! Don't mumble!

AMALIA. Eva Perón, Nonna. What is it, Aunt Paula?

PAULA. *(Laughing.)* Nothing. I don't know ...

AMALIA. / Pills, dear ...

MADDALENA. / Always somebody dying in this country. All this death ... and the mumbling ... Nobody ever died in San Germano. And nobody mumbled. *(Shouting.)* We 'ave no secrets! (/ *Elena changes stations. All have the same broadcast.)*

RADIO. *(V.O.)* ... *as the city slowly grinds to a stop. Crowds are already forming in front of the presidential palace. Several road blocks have already gone up and more are expected.* / *The president respectfully asks the population to stay calm. As store signs and street lights are dimmed in mourning, the National Guard has been called to patrol the streets together with the police to help maintain order so that no unseemly disturbances mar the solemnity of this tragic day.* *(Paula starts laughing again.)*

ELENA. / (Overlap.) Aunt Paula, Nonna, I better take you home.

MADDALENA. To Piemonte?

ELENA. Clara, shall I give you a lift to the hotel? You won't find a cab.

CLARA. (Gathering her things.) Thank you.

RADIO. (V.O.) … candlelight vigils have started in most quarters of the city. Father Benítez, who was called to administer last rites at three o'clock this afternoon, is leading a crowd of mourners in the Rosary on the steps of the cathedral and all neighborhood churches have followed suit with Requiem masses and rosaries as people gather to pray for Eva Perón's eternal rest.

OTTO. (Helping them into their raincoats.) Go straight home. Call the minute you arrive. You too, Aunt Clara. If for any reason you're stopped, say you're going to the nearest church. (Elena, Clara and Paula exit, taking Maddalena and ad-libbing goodbyes. Otto walks them out.)

MADDALENA. (Offstage.) Where am I going? I just got here!

CLARA. (Offstage.) / Alsatians?

PAULA. (Offstage.) That's what they say …

RADIO. (V.O.) / Millions of bereaved Argentines are expected to pass before the body which will lie in state at the Ministry of Labor for two weeks so the people can present their respects and express their profound grief on the face of this irreparable loss for the nation and for our leader, General Juan Domingo Perón. (/ Rosa enters from the kitchen.)

ROSA. Dead, is she.

AMALIA. Come along, Lise. I'll make you chocolate and whipped cream and we'll listen to Tarzan on the radio.

ROSA. They cancelled all the programs. I'll take her. Here, we'll play a game of checkers, and you can cheat. (Rosa and Lise 2 exit hand in hand.)

LISE. How did you know?

ROSA. I pay attention.

LISE 2. (Offstage. On their way out.) Am I gonna die?

ROSA. (Offstage.) 'Course not.

LISE 2. Are you?

ROSA. (Offstage.) No, no …

LISE 2. (Offstage.) Is Papi?

LISE. Soon … of cigarettes and loss … (Otto reenters.)

AMALIA. You've been out looking for him, haven't you?

OTTO. Who?

AMALIA. That boy. Santo. Is that what you've been doing all these nights you've been coming home so late? Looking for that boy? *(Pause.)*

OTTO. When I first saw him huddled in that kitchen chair — a month ago, is it? — I said to him: "Santo, my friend," I called him that, can you imagine? "I sympathize with your position, I even agree with it, but ... you can't stay ... I've got my family in there, you see ... my wife, my children ... you must go. I'm sorry." And I went back to the table and there we all were ... eating cake ... And I — I ... *(Amalia lights a cigarette and goes to the radio. She flips through the dial. A priest in public broadcast will chant the "De Profundis" under the following.)*

RADIO. *(V.O.)*

> */ De profundis clamavi ad te Domine*
> *Domine, exaudi vocem meam.*
> *Fiant aures tuae intendentes ...*
> *... in vocem deprecationis meae.*
> *Si iniquitates observaveris, Domine:*
> *Domine, quis sustinebit?*
> *Quia apud te propitiatio est:*
> *... et propter legem tuam sustinui, te, Domine.*
> *Sustinuit anima mea in verbo ejus:*
> *... speravit anima mea in Domino.*
> *A custodia matutina usque ad noctem: speret Israel in Domino.*
> *Quia apud Dominum misericordia: et copiosa apud eum redemptio.*

LISE. */ (Over the "De Profundis." To audience.)* This — *small* incident — This man I don't even remember, seems to have — *(To her parents.)* It was *safer* than this! I remember it *safe.* It *felt* safe!

AMALIA. It was never *safe!*

OTTO. In Vienna too, we, all *good people,* thought we could sit it out — the advancing disaster, the "house painter" — playing Schubert and sipping *Kaffee mit Schlag.* Windows and doors locked airtight. And then the *boogeyman* came calling at the gate and nothing was ever familiar again.

LISE. That's not how you used to remember it! You loved Vienna!

OTTO. I didn't *know* Vienna!

LISE. So what?! Why do you have to *know* what you love?

OTTO. *(Quietly.)* It's about *us,* don't you see. *We* were not who we said we were.

LISE. *(Frantic.)* No! This is — This isn't — It's — It's — *(Pause.)*

OTTO. In the street tonight, elbow to elbow with the *unfamiliar* again, in the midst of all those candles — candles everywhere — fire in the rain ... I tried very hard — I thought if at least I could *understand* this — this real or imagined grief, I —

LISE. You wanted to join *that* mob?

AMALIA. Leave it to you to romanticize mass hysteria.

LISE. Were you wrong about *everything?*

OTTO. I don't know. They were united, "one," and look at me: / a stranger everywhere ...

LISE. ... / a stranger everywhere ...

AMALIA. What about your family?

OTTO. It's not enough.

LISE. Not enough...?

AMALIA. What are we supposed to do? We're not — we're just — we're common, *ordinary people!* What do expect us to *do! (Lise 2 appears at the door.)*

LISE 2. Is Uncle H coming over tonight?

OTTO. *He's not your uncle!* He's an intruder who — (/ *Lise 2 disappears quickly.)*

AMALIA. / Otto!

LISE. This man, this *Santo,* this *ghost,* was the *intruder* in this house. *(Beat.)* You weren't happy?

OTTO. Happy? I'm Viennese.

LISE. That's not funny.

OTTO. Oh, unhappiness can be profoundly comical, monkey-face. *(Upstage, Lise 2 and Rosa cross in the hall on their way to bed.)*

LISE. *(To Lise 2.)* Are *you* unhappy?

LISE 2. *(Without stopping.)* What's "unhappy"?

ROSA. Bedtime.

LISE 2. *(Offstage. On their way out.)* I'm not doing any dying.

ROSA. *(Offstage.)* No, no ...

LISE 2. *(Offstage.)* What's "unhappy"?

OTTO. *"And all the king's soldiers, and all the king's men ... "* *(Amalia turns off the radio.)*

AMALIA. *(Matter-of-fact.)* My mother had white peacocks in the garden. One night when I was a child, one of the field hands' fighting cocks got out and killed them all. We found them at sunrise on the green with their throats cut. Snow-white feathers dripping blood on the grass, and the sun coming up. Poor, useless, vain creatures couldn't even manage to live in peace. Please, Otto, no grandstands. Nothing changes and we'll end up burying you. This has nothing to do with us. It's just politics. Nothing to do with us. *(She exits. Pause. Otto crosses to piano and starts gathering the piano scores. He clutches them to his chest.)*

71

OTTO. Where did I leave my umbrella, I wonder ... *(He pulls up a piano score. To Lise.) Madama Butterfly.* Signed by Puccini himself. Did I ever tell you he once smoked a cigar in my grandfather's club?
LISE. No, you didn't.
OTTO. Really? Perhaps there wasn't enough time. Perhaps it never happened. *(He starts out.)*
LISE. Dad!
OTTO. *"Dad"?*
LISE. ... *Papi* ...
OTTO. Now I know me ... *(He exits.)*
LISE. Wait!
AMALIA. *(Crossing upstage with a crystal bowl of fresh violets.)* Nothing to worry about, darling. Why don't you practice a little piano? *(Automatically Lise crosses to the piano. Amalia starts straightening the room.)*
LISE. But ... I'm not there anymore ...
AMALIA. Everything's perfectly all right ...
LISE. ... am I?
AMALIA. Why don't you play a little piano ...
LISE. And you? Were you also —
AMALIA. It was a very happy home ...
LISE. Why don't I know you better?
AMALIA. *(On her way out.)* Keep a flexible wrist, dear ... *(Lise starts playing "Für Elise." Amalia exits, humming along. Lise 2 joins Lise at the piano.)*

Scene 2

Lise 2 at the piano, "learning" "Für Elise." Henri paces.

HENRI. Uruguay? That tiny little country? What on earth for?
OTTO. Easier to keep an eye on the borders. *(They laugh.)* No, I've been offered an excellent job in a new engineering firm.
HENRI. Why not stay and build *us* a few bridges? We *need* men like you.
OTTO. "Men like me"?
HENRI. *(Guardedly.)* Good men.

72

OTTO. Ah … "good" … yes …

HENRI. You'd be part of a nation reinventing itself.

OTTO. I never quite got the knack of being a *part* of anything, I'm afraid.

HENRI. The right people would make a difference. The problem is always in the beginning. Beginnings are — awkward.

OTTO. Beginning … what … exactly …

HENRI. To catch up with the rest of the world. With history.

OTTO. Heady stuff, history. *(Beat.)* Alberto says Argentines don't love Argentina, but I think you do.

HENRI. Yes.

OTTO. More than people?

HENRI. More than individuals, yes. *(Pause.)*

OTTO. *(Kindly.)* Buenos Aires has the widest avenues in the world, did you know?

HENRI. *(Pleased.)* Do we really? *(Pause. Thunder.)* Who will I visit on evenings like this?

OTTO. You have many friends.

HENRI. I know many people. *(Pause. Thunder.)*

OTTO. Filthy weather.

HENRI. Tough winter.

OTTO. *(Beat.)* Is Angelica still at her parents'? *(Pause.)*

HENRI. Men with — "causes" shouldn't have families. *(Laughing.)* They should borrow them. Like me. *(Pause.)*

OTTO. *Can* you get us the passports?

HENRI. Of course.

OTTO. When?

HENRI. In a hurry? Sorry, I don't mean to pry.

OTTO. It's always hard to leave. Best do it quickly.

HENRI. You're afraid of something.

OTTO. No … *(Offstage, service doorbell and Rosa's voice.)*

HENRI. *Nothing* would ever happen to you. You know that, don't you? You would always be — safe.

OTTO. *Safe? (Alberto enters unannounced. Offstage, the piano stops.)*

ALBERTO. Ah. You have company. I'll —

OTTO. Something wrong?

ALBERTO. I'll come back.

OTTO. No, no, come in.

ALBERTO. *(Beat.)* No, really, I just — is Elena here? I went by her apartment. I thought she might be —

73

OTTO. She's skiing in Bariloche.

ALBERTO. Well, then I'll —

HENRI. I heard about the newspaper. I'm sorry. / If you need —

ALBERTO. / Are you.

OTTO. / (Topping.) What about the paper?

ALBERTO. (To Henri.) Tell him.

OTTO. What ...

ALBERTO. (To Otto.) Ask your *friend* here.

OTTO. I don't —

ALBERTO. I didn't require the personnel to go to "The Funeral" and the fuckers shut me down!

HENRI. I understand it's temporary. It'll be printing again next month.

ALBERTO. Under whose direction?

HENRI. This is not a discussion we need to have here, Alberto.

ALBERTO. Why? Afraid to pop the bubble?

OTTO. What are you doing, Alberto?

HENRI. (Steady.) The activities of "your" paper have been temporarily suspended because of irresponsible journalism on your part. Until the Labor situation is stabilized —

ALBERTO. My paper was shut down because it reported extensively on strikes initiated by non-state-approved unions and on the police action which put a stop to them.

HENRI. Let's not talk politics here.

ALBERTO. Why? What's so special about this house that you can't bring politics into it? What's wrong, the house or the politics?

HENRI. I don't like making scenes in other people's homes.

ALBERTO. Especially this one, right? Sanctuary! Sanctuary! Here one talks only of the diminished seventh and the iambic pentameter!

HENRI. It's late. You're going to wake up the entire family.

ALBERTO. About time! You feel like a decent man here, don't you?

HENRI. You've put over three hundred people out of work! Do you want to take *everyone else* down with you? Is that what you came here to do?

ALBERTO. I came because I can't use my phone anymore. I don't remember what it's like to walk around, or to stop for coffee somewhere, without being followed. Look out the window. I'm sure you'll recognize the two goons from your department pretending to wait for the bus at the corner.

HENRI. I warned you a long time ago. / We're trying to rebuild a nation, not a boys' club!

ALBERTO. / *(To Otto.)* Let me make sure we all know who we are: This man works for a regime which routinely uses clandestine arrest, torture and murder against *any* opposition in the name of national security and social progress. Any more family birthdays you would like him to come to? Who knows, *he* may have a couple of book burnings you might like to attend? *(Pause.)*

OTTO. *(Quietly.)* I can't do this — what you want me to do, Alberto. I am not a political individual. I don't want to change the world. I want to live *privately* and in peace.

ALBERTO. *In peace?* Do you know that Santo Arrúa was picked up leaving your house on the night of June twenty-four? They followed him here, you see, but they had orders —

HENRI. *(Overlap.)* Shut up!

ALBERTO. — *orders* not to come in. Not to disrupt your *peace.* So they waited. And they got him. Piece of cake. *(Pause.)*

HENRI. *(Quietly.)* You stupid, *stupid,* destructive bastard.

OTTO. *(To Henri.)* You arrested a man leaving my house?

HENRI. I had nothing to do with it and it has nothing to do with you. You don't even know him.

OTTO. But I do. I do know him. He's Rosa's brother.

HENRI. That won't be a problem. It was your daughter's birthday, and —

OTTO. You're wrong. I would have helped him if ... if only ... *(Pause.)*

HENRI. Do you think you would have gotten very far?

OTTO. Why, are you having me watched too? *(Pause. Both Lises appear at the door.)*

HENRI. Good work, Alberto.

LISE 2. Uncle H! Wanna come and read *Alice* with me?

HENRI. Not now, sweetheart.

LISE 2. But —

OTTO. Lise, go to your room! *(She exits quickly but Lise stays.)*

ALBERTO. That little girl's the only one here who doesn't *know* you, Henri. The love of a child is an invaluable thing. Don't bother sending the boys to my house. I won't be there. And I've taken the cat. The rest you can torch. Oh, and my mother is a Basque and the widow of an army colonel. I would stay clear of her. *(To Otto.)* I came to tell you I'll be away for a while. *(He exits. Silence.)*

OTTO. What happened to Santo Arrúa, Henri?

HENRI. I thought you weren't interested in politics.

OTTO. *What happened to Santo Arrúa?*

HENRI. *(The truth.)* I don't know. You'll have your passports tomorrow. *(Amalia enters.)*

AMALIA. Henri, Lise says you can't leave without —

HENRI. I'm sorry. I'm expected somewhere. Give her my love. *(He starts off. Stops.)* I am not a violent man. I have honestly, *passionately* wanted to — serve — to be of public service. To help change — The crime rate has dropped by forty percent. Women can walk out at night alone without … without … Jesus …

OTTO. *(Quietly.)* … and all the trains run on time…? *(Silence.)*

HENRI. *(Quietly.)* Surely there will be — understanding for mistakes made in good faith … *(Silence.)* I thank you both for the time you've *lavished* on me all these years.

OTTO. It's we who —

HENRI. No, no. It was easy. A word. Really. Not for you, I imagine. *(Beat.)* Were you / afraid all the time?

LISE. / *(Realization.)* … afraid all the time…!

OTTO.   AMALIA.
No.   Oh, no!

OTTO. Yes. But there's been no pretense. Ever.

HENRI. And now you find you … can't anymore. *(Silence.)* Good night. *(Lise 2 reappears with Rosa behind her who stays by the door. She runs to Henri.)*

LISE 2. You're leaving?

HENRI. I'm sorry, princess, I have to.

LISE 2. You're coming back later?

HENRI. Not today, darling.

LISE 2. Tomorrow then?

HENRI. *(Beat.)* Good night.

LISE 2. *(Grabbing his sleeve, sensing something's very wrong.)* Tomorrow?

HENRI. You'll be going — going on a boat trip, soon. Did you know?

LISE 2. A boat trip?

HENRI. Oh, yes. Great fun. You'll have to watch out for pirates though.

LISE 2. *(Apprehensive.)* Pirates…?

LISE. Ghosts …

HENRI. Black mast …

LISE and HENRI. … red sails …

ROSA and HENRI. *(At door.)* … a ghost ship … *(Sound. The distant horn call of* The Flying Dutchman. *Rosa and Henri look at each*

76

other a long moment.)
LISE 2. Are you coming too?
HENRI. I ... [*can't*] ...
LISE. Was that it? I was just a kid and didn't ask difficult questions?
LISE 2. Am — am I your best buddy...? *(Henri turns to leave.)* I thought you loved me...! *(He stops a second, then continues out. To her parents, tears and rage.)* What did you *do* to him? *(She turns and runs out in tears. She's intercepted by Rosa who picks her up. Offstage, front door closing.)*
LISE. *(To Rosa.)* He told me stories, he brought me books, he ... *(In Henri's direction.)* I — [*loved you*] — was never afraid! *(Rose exits with Lise 2.)*
AMALIA. What happened? *(Pause. Door closes offstage.)*
OTTO. I think I know what the devil wanted.
AMALIA. The devil?
OTTO. Yes. I never understood the idea of the devil because I couldn't imagine what he could possibly want. Power? He had that. Immortality? He had that too. But I've been thinking: goodness he didn't have. Maybe he wanted *goodness*. *(Lights. Tango music "Mi Buenos Aires Querido." As in the beginning. In a spot Lise dances a few tango steps. Then gives up.)*
LISE. *(To audience.)* You see the trouble with nostalgia is — the trouble is — nostalgia —

EPILOGUE

Ship horn. The docks again. Night. A haze of cigarette smoke. As at the beginning, there is the silhouette of a transatlantic liner. Ship whistles are heard intermittently during the scene. Amalia, Elena and Otto. Amalia has a bunch of fresh violets pinned on her lapel.

ELENA. *(Smoking.)* Where are they?

AMALIA. There's time.

OTTO. Not much. Got everything you need?

ELENA. Oh, yes. I'll be spending Christmas in winter. Ridiculous!

OTTO. Passport? Tickets? Visas?

ELENA. All here. *(Beat.)* Did he get my papers too? *(No answer.)* We can't escape being indebted to the man, can we. *(Beat.)* When do you go?

OTTO. Next week. Any word from Alberto?

ELENA. Nothing. His mother hasn't heard, or won't say.

AMALIA. You're going see the New Look first hand. Lucky girl.

OTTO. Will you be able to get work there?

ELENA. Maybe. *(Beat.)* It wasn't just the politics that kept me from going back on stage, you know. I lost my nerve. What kind of actor goes on stage with nothing to die for and no one to kill? I'm a fraud. I should do movies. *(Ship whistle again. Maddalena, hat askew and wild-eyed, enters followed by Juan, and Paula.)*

PAULA. Sorry we're late. There was a — *(A glance at Maddalena.)* a little hitch.

JUAN. *(Exhausted.)* She misunderstood. We had to unpack her.

PAULA. First we had to pry her off the steamer trunk.

AMALIA. Are you all right, Nonna?

MADDALENA. How should I be all right? They stole all my clothes! Where everybody going?

JUAN. Everybody is *not* going. *We're* staying.

MADDALENA. I don't want to. *(She digs in her enormous black handbag.)* Got my papers here. See? And my passport. I never make citizen so I can get away.

78

JUAN. We know, *Mamma.* Nevertheless.

ELENA. She wants to go, she stays. I want to stay, I go.

MADDALENA. Where she going, the actress?

ELENA. Nonna, do you think you could talk to me directly just this once? I'm going away.

MADDALENA. We *been* away, years now.

ELENA. Well, give me a kiss.

MADDALENA. *(To the others.)* She better not slobber on me like Labrador. *(She whacks Elena across the shins with her cane.)*

ELENA. *(Hopping.)* There is this *myth* about Italians being warm-hearted.

MADDALENA. *(Looking straight ahead.)* Where she going?

ELENA. Paris.

MADDALENA. Full of tarts.

OTTO. And Argentines ...

MADDALENA. Same *ting.* What she do there?

ELENA. That thing you don't like, Nonna. Theatre. If they'll have me.

MADDALENA. What she mean, "have her"?

ELENA. They may not like me.

MADDALENA. *(Outraged.)* You the best!

ELENA. *(Beat.)* What...?

JUAN. Don't get your hopes up. It's the pack instinct. She feels the same way about Lucky Luciano.

ELENA. Nonna: come with me!

ALL. *(Ad-lib.)* Come on Elena! / Don't start! / You'll get her all riled up!

ELENA. I mean it. Screw Paris. We'll go to San Germano. We'll watch those sheep beetling back and forth across the Appenines sunup to sundown. What do you say? Show me that passport. *(The boat whistle is heard. Maddalena fumbles with the catch of her handbag and can't get it open again. Pause. She looks at her arthritic hands.)*

MADDALENA. I ... too old. *(Bewildered.)* How I get so old so soon?

ELENA. I guess time flies when you're pissed off, Nonna.

MADDALENA. *(Beat.)* I not borned pissed off. I get pissed off later. *(Pause.)* When you come back, *mmmaybe* I go see you on the st— on the st— *(Choking on the word.)* — stage! *(Pause. Everybody stares at her in disbelief.)*

PAULA. What —?

MADDALENA. *(To Elena.)* I not go all this time because I am so nervous — I shake. And my teeth make a noise and then they fall out.

PAULA. *(Seething.)* Fifty years ago she told me she'd see me *dead* in a coffin rather than on a stage!

MADDALENA. *(Beat.)* People change.

PAULA. *NOT GODDAMN FAST ENOUGH!*

JUAN.   AMALIA.   ELENA.

Paula!   Calm down, darling.   Upstaged again …

PAULA. Don't you tell me — *Fifty years* I — I couldn't even take dance *lessons* —

MADDALENA. See? A lunatic. Carry on like that all day. About nothing.

PAULA. *Nothing?* / *Nothing?*

MADDALENA. / Don't be silly. She was always silly.

PAULA. You thought I had no talent! Was that it?

MADDALENA. I'm your mother. I protect you.

PAULA. You thought I'd make a fool of myself! I've thrown my life away on a woman who's / always thought me ridiculous!

AMALIA.   ELENA.

/ Shhhhh! Please!   Nonna, Paula! I'm *leaving! THE
                                 COUNTRY! (Sotto.)* Fuck me …

MADDALENA. *(To the others.)* She have nasty temper, that Paula. Where she get that? / Nobody else in the family —

JUAN. / *(Overlapping.)* Come on, Paula. She's old, it's all right now. It's all water under the bridge. *(What follows is a dreadful public fight where Paula and Maddalena have to be physically restrained from going at each other, with everybody shouting at once.)*

PAULA. *(Hysterical.)* Well it's my goddamn bridge and it's not "all right"! It'll never be "all right"! There are things that never get to be "*all right*"! What are you, an American?

JUAN. *(Exploding.)* I wish to hell I was! Why do you think they're doing so well? They're *optimists!* A sunny people! Everything's OK! This fucking country! What went wrong here?

OTTO. *(To Juan.)* I thought you liked it here.

JUAN. I do! I don't get it! / The eternal gloom and doom! The tango, where everybody dies, or runs away and *then* dies! / And then the *widows* keen, and the *orphans* wail, and there's another *tango! Mannaggia!* Shoot me. Somebody shoot me, please!

AMALIA. / Please, people are staring. We're making a scene …

MADDALENA. / *(Innocently.)* Why everybody shouting?

ELENA.   AMALIA.

/ Papa, please!   Shhhhh!

LISE. *(Suddenly in the middle of the fray.)* Stop it, everybody! Stop!

This is SO embarrassing! SHUT UP! *(To audience.)* It was a very happy home!

PAULA. He was always the favorite! He could do anything he wanted! He was a *BOY!*

MADDALENA. See? Crazy! La Pavlova, she never see her! She have the measles when we go, *she* stay home! She never see her! Not once!

PAULA. *(Shrieking.)* I saw her! I saw her! I saw her!

MADDALENA. *(To Paula.)* End up in the madhouse, girl.

LISE. She did. After putting the contents of the catbox in Nonna's coffee, one gray winter morning. *(Ship horn.)*

MADDALENA. Time to go away yet? *(Elena tries to put her arms around her. She whacks her across the shins again with her cane.)* And don't *touch* alla time! *(The ship's horn is heard again. Maddalena gasps and puts a fist to her chest.)*

JUAN. What, *Mamma*, what?

MADDALENA. Icepick through the heart. / Lilac in the afternoon ... what...? *(/ Clara enters in traveling clothes.)*

CLARA. It's the last call, Elena. *(She kisses everybody quickly and exits.)*

LISE. Elena wouldn't come back and everybody knew it, but incredibly, for people who could say "goodbye" in several languages, I never once heard them say the word.

AMALIA. Paris violets are most beautiful in the fall.

ELENA. Yes. But they're smaller. *Ciao. (She blows them all a kiss and quickly walks away.)*

MADDALENA. *(Bellowing.)* You have warm socks? REMEMBER *TITANIC!*

ALL. *(Ad-lib. Outraged.)* Christ! / Really! / God's sake! / *Mother!* / Of all the things to say! / Unbelievable! *(Etc., etc.)*

LISE. Ten years later they would all tumble into an airport in the same dishevelled, irritating way, this time to see *me* off. For good. They didn't know that. I did. For a second there I looked at my father's pale face and already frail frame and — but the Pan Am jet gleamed silver on the runway, poised for take-off, in the act almost ... and I headed north ... where such things as midnight flights, safe conducts, exit permits, special visas, barbed wire, night patrols, are the stuff of black-and-white movies and where fascist dictatorships become Broadway musicals and there is no boogeyman. And everything is OK. *(Beat.) I'm* not an exile. *(Beat.)* Am I? *(A spot on Lise 2 in traveling clothes, hat, coat, gloves, phone in hand.)*

LISE 2. Hello? Is this Marco Dormanowicz? This is the secret police — *(Rosa picks her up in mid-sentence and carries her out.)* Arggghhh!

(Offstage, in the dark.) Hell.

LISE. Soon after, little Uruguay, legendarily democratic, went "the way of the generals" too and, there was one more flight, this time without Papi and the piano scores, but I wasn't there. In yet another country, my mother retains the vague, unsure manner of foreigners and people who have come great distances, and I wonder whether she remembers what I remember but am afraid to ask. Some late afternoons when we have a Cinzano together and she sits on my sofa playing with her little dog I try surreptitiously and in vain to find traces of the great beauty that was. Only the unexpected scent of violets can bring it back. *(Beat.)* Proust knew everything too. My father died young. One day, after that jet plane had taken me as far away as I could get, even his music failed him and he was alone in that last, most absolute silence. Like him, I smoke when I'm sad. *(She checks her pockets for cigarettes she doesn't have.)* Shit. *(Beat.)* The details of his face often escape me now but always, in the catch of the strings when I hear an orchestra tuning in the pit, I find again the distinctive crackle of his voice, and in the exploding Strauss waltz, the treacherous, paralyzing pull of nostalgia for that dazzling ballroom implicit in all our conversations, which, idealizing his own past, he accidentally and almost fatally, intimated one day would contain *me*. You see, the trouble with nostalgia is, it completes the incomplete, and so, it lies ... and ... and I'm afraid nothing remembered is really true, and ... *(Beat.)* Still ... something about the way I *see* things ... is ... isn't — *(Music — "The Rosenkavalier Waltz." Far upstage Otto and Lise 2 waltz as flames flicker on the walls. After the first full "statement" of the waltz Lise 2 retreats into the dark. Otto turns to Lise. She puts her arms out to waltz with him. He recedes into the dark. The waltz dissolves into the "Magic Fire" music. Lise stands in the center alone. The lights go out one by one. A flash: Henri's face as he lights his cigarette. Lights.)*

End of Play

SUPPLEMENTARY RADIO ANNOUNCEMENT
FOR ACT THREE, SCENE 1

The executive branch of the Eva Perón Foundation as well as prominent leaders of the CGT are at this moment arriving at the presidential palace, to be received by members of the Cabinet also already in transit. National police escorts have been provided for all members of foreign embassies and consulates, cultural attachés and diplomats making their way to the presidential palace, as circulation is heavily hindered by the crowds in the streets. Mounted police has tripled in number and has requested, most especially, that people keep children and the elderly away from the horses to avoid incident.

Farmer representatives of the Agrarian Federation of Argentina are expected to arrive tomorrow. Among those already here: representatives from Santa Fe, Cordoba, Mendoza and La Plata. To facilitate their arrival — and that of other mourning citizens from the provinces, railway and autobus services are kept running exclusively for that purpose. All other commercial uses of national and private means of public transportation are temporarily suspended, as well as all commercial and mercantile enterprise. Police corps delegations from all districts in the provinces are also expected to arrive in the early hours of the afternoon tomorrow, July twenty-seventh.

PROPERTY LIST

Zenith radio
Phonograph, records
Bar with glasses and several bottles of liquor, wine and
    champagne
Full dinner service (Act Two)
Cigarette, lighter (LISE, ELENA, AMALIA)
Phone (LISE)
Old suitcases (GIOVANNI)
Suitcase, Olivetti (OTTO)
Valkyrie helmet made from newspaper (LISE 2)
Wrap, gloves (AMALIA)
Folded newspaper (ELENA, AMALIA)
Two paperback books (ALBERTO)
Bowl of nuts (OTTO)
Purse with pillbox (PAULA)
Violets (HENRI)
Violets on lapel (AMALIA)
Crystal bowl with violets (AMALIA)
Book (LISE 2)
Chocolate truffles (HENRI)
Large headless doll in red dress (LISE 2)
Tablecloth (LISE 2)
Coffee, cigarettes (OTTO and HENRI)
Bread and jam (LISE 2)
Basket of bread (AMALIA)
Bowls of pasta (ROSA)
Salad (ROSA)
Gift-wrapped book (HENRI)
Velvet box with white lace fan (CLARA)
Tall broom with large red bow (ELENA)
Chocolate cake with candles (ROSA)
Coffee pot (AMALIA)
Cigar (JUAN)
Crochet (CLARA)
Book, crayons (LISE 2)
Tea tray with sachertorte and tea service, cake knife (AMALIA
    and ROSA)
Piano scores (OTTO)
Handbag, cane (MADDALENA)

SOUND EFFECTS

"Mi Buenos Aires Querido"
Transatlantic steamer horn
Zither intro from Strauss' *Tales from the Vienna Woods*
Waltz from Strauss' *Tales from the Vienna Woods*
Richard Tauber singing "Leise, ganz leise" from *Watzertraum*
Franco Corelli singing "Cuore 'ngrato"
End of Act One duet from *La Boheme*
Prelude to *Das Rheingold*
"Magic Fire" music from end of *Die Walkure*
Trucks, shouts of "Peron!"
Horn call of *The Flying Dutchman*
Tosca — end of Act Three
"Ride of the Valkyries" — played one key at a time
"Brindisi" from *La Traviata* (a Callas version)
Police disturbance
Police sirens
Door buzzer
Bastianini singing "Il Balen" from *Trovatore*
Car doors slamming
Fireworks
"Por Una Cabeza"
Pistol shots
Tauber singing "Wien du Stadt meiner Traume"
"Flower Duet" from *Madama Butterfly*
Radio broadcasts about Eva Peron's death
Chopin's "Funeral March"
"Für Elise"
Thunder
Ship whistles
"The Rosencavalier Waltz"

NEW PLAYS

★ **THE EXONERATED by Jessica Blank and Erik Jensen.** Six interwoven stories paint a picture of an American criminal justice system gone horribly wrong and six brave souls who persevered to survive it. "The #1 play of the year...intense and deeply affecting..." *–NY Times.* "Riveting. Simple, honest storytelling that demands reflection." *–A.P.* "Artful and moving...pays tribute to the resilience of human hearts and minds." *–Variety.* "Stark...riveting...cunningly orchestrated." *–The New Yorker.* "Hard-hitting, powerful, and socially relevant." *–Hollywood Reporter.* [7M, 3W] ISBN: 0-8222-1946-8

★ **STRING FEVER by Jacquelyn Reingold.** Lily juggles the big issues: turning forty, artificial insemination and the elusive scientific Theory of Everything in this Off-Broadway comedy hit. "Applies the elusive rules of string theory to the conundrums of one woman's love life. Think *Sex and the City* meets *Copenhagen.*" *–NY Times.* "A funny offbeat and touching look at relationships...an appealing romantic comedy populated by oddball characters." *–NY Daily News.* "Where kooky, zany, and madcap meet...whimsically winsome." *–NY Magazine.* "STRING FEVER will have audience members happily stringing along." *–TheaterMania.com.* "Reingold's language is surprising, inventive, and unique." *–nytheatre.com.* "...[a] whimsical comic voice." *–Time Out.* [3M, 3W (doubling)] ISBN: 0-8222-1952-2

★ **DEBBIE DOES DALLAS adapted by Erica Schmidt, composed by Andrew Sherman, conceived by Susan L. Schwartz.** A modern morality tale told as a comic musical of tragic proportions as the classic film is brought to the stage. "A scream! A saucy, tongue-in-cheek romp." *–The New Yorker.* "Hilarious! DEBBIE manages to have it all: beauty, brains and a great sense of humor!" *–Time Out.* "Shamelessly silly, shrewdly self-aware and proud of being naughty. Great fun!" *–NY Times.* "Racy and raucous, a lighthearted, fast-paced thoroughly engaging and hilarious send-up." *–NY Daily News.* [3M, 5W] ISBN: 0-8222-1955-7

★ **THE MYSTERY PLAYS by Roberto Aguirre-Sacasa.** Two interrelated one acts, loosely based on the tradition of the medieval mystery plays. "... stylish, spine-tingling...Mr. Aguirre-Sacasa uses standard tricks of horror stories, borrowing liberally from masters like Kafka, Lovecraft, Hitchcock...But his mastery of the genre is his own...irresistible." *–NY Times.* "Undaunted by the special-effects limitations of theatre, playwright and *Marvel* comic-book writer Roberto Aguirre-Sacasa maps out some creepy twilight zones in THE MYSTERY PLAYS, an engaging, related pair of one acts...The theatre may rarely deliver shocks equivalent to, say, *Dawn of the Dead*, but Aguirre-Sacasa's work is fine compensation." *–Time Out.* [4M, 2W] ISBN: 0-8222-2038-5

★ **THE JOURNALS OF MIHAIL SEBASTIAN by David Auburn.** This epic one-man play spans eight tumultuous years and opens a uniquely personal window on the Romanian Holocaust and the Second World War. "Powerful." *–NY Times.* "[THE JOURNALS OF MIHAIL SEBASTIAN] allows us to glimpse the idiosyncratic effects of that awful history on one intelligent, pragmatic, recognizably real man..." *–NY Newsday.* [3M, 5W] ISBN: 0-8222-2006-0

★ **LIVING OUT by Lisa Loomer.** The story of the complicated relationship between a Salvadoran nanny and the Anglo lawyer she works for. "A stellar new play. Searingly funny." *–The New Yorker.* "Both generous and merciless, equally enjoyable and disturbing." *–NY Newsday.* "A bitingly funny new comedy. The plight of working mothers is explored from two pointedly contrasting perspectives in this sympathetic, sensitive new play." *–Variety.* [2M, 6W] ISBN: 0-8222-1994-8

DRAMATISTS PLAY SERVICE, INC.
440 Park Avenue South, New York, NY 10016 212-683-8960 Fax 212-213-1539
postmaster@dramatists.com   www.dramatists.com

NEW PLAYS

★ **MATCH by Stephen Belber.** Mike and Lisa Davis interview a dancer and choreographer about his life, but it is soon evident that their agenda will either ruin or inspire them— and definitely change their lives forever. "Prolific laughs and ear-to-ear smiles." *–NY Magazine.* "Uproariously funny, deeply moving, enthralling theater. Stephen Belber's MATCH has great beauty and tenderness, and abounds in wit." *–NY Daily News.* "Three and a half out of four stars." *–USA Today.* "A theatrical steeplechase that leads straight from outrageous bitchery to unadorned, heartfelt emotion." *–Wall Street Journal.* [2M, 1W] ISBN: 0-8222-2020-2

★ **HANK WILLIAMS: LOST HIGHWAY by Randal Myler and Mark Harelik.** The story of the beloved and volatile country-music legend Hank Williams, featuring twenty-five of his most unforgettable songs. "[LOST HIGHWAY has] the exhilarating feeling of Williams on stage in a particular place on a particular night…serves up classic country with the edges raw and the energy hot…By the end of the play, you've traveled on a profound emotional journey: LOST HIGHWAY transports its audience and communicates the inspiring message of the beauty and richness of Williams' songs…forceful, clear-eyed, moving, impressive." *–Rolling Stone.* "…honors a very particular musical talent with care and energy… smart, sweet, poignant." *–NY Times.* [7M, 3W] ISBN: 0-8222-1985-9

★ **THE STORY by Tracey Scott Wilson.** An ambitious black newspaper reporter goes against her editor to investigate a murder and finds the *best* story…but at what cost? "A singular new voice…deeply emotional, deeply intellectual, and deeply musical…" *–The New Yorker.* "…a conscientious and absorbing new drama…" *–NY Times.* "…a riveting, tough-minded drama about race, reporting and the truth…" *–A.P.* "… a stylish, attention-holding script that ends on a chilling note that will leave viewers with much to talk about." *–Curtain Up.* [2M, 7W (doubling, flexible casting)] ISBN: 0-8222-1998-0

★ **OUR LADY OF 121st STREET by Stephen Adly Guirgis.** The body of Sister Rose, beloved Harlem nun, has been stolen, reuniting a group of life-challenged childhood friends who square off as they wait for her return. "A scorching and dark new comedy… Mr. Guirgis has one of the finest imaginations for dialogue to come along in years." *–NY Times.* "Stephen Guirgis may be the best playwright in America under forty." *–NY Magazine.* [8M, 4W] ISBN: 0-8222-1965-4

★ **HOLLYWOOD ARMS by Carrie Hamilton and Carol Burnett.** The coming-of-age story of a dreamer who manages to escape her bleak life and follow her romantic ambitions to stardom. Based on Carol Burnett's bestselling autobiography, *One More Time.* "…pure theatre and pure entertainment…" *–Talkin' Broadway.* "…a warm, fuzzy evening of theatre." *–BrodwayBeat.com.* "…chuckles and smiles of recognition or surprise flow naturally…a remarkable slice of life." *–TheatreScene.net.* [5M, 5W, 1 girl] ISBN: 0-8222-1959-X

★ **INVENTING VAN GOGH by Steven Dietz.** A haunting and hallucinatory drama about the making of art, the obsession to create and the fine line that separates truth from myth. "Like a van Gogh painting, Dietz's story is a gorgeous example of excess—one that remakes reality with broad, well-chosen brush strokes. At evening's end, we're left with the author's resounding opinions on art and artifice, and provoked by his constant query into which is greater: van Gogh's art or his violent myth." *–Phoenix New Times.* "Dietz's writing is never simple. It is always brilliant. Shaded, compressed, direct, lucid—he frames his subject with a remarkable understanding of painting as a physical experience." *–Tucson Citizen.* [4M, 1W] ISBN: 0-8222-1954-9

DRAMATISTS PLAY SERVICE, INC.
440 Park Avenue South, New York, NY 10016 212-683-8960 Fax 212-213-1539
postmaster@dramatists.com www.dramatists.com

NEW PLAYS

★ **INTIMATE APPAREL by Lynn Nottage.** The moving and lyrical story of a turn-of-the-century black seamstress whose gifted hands and sewing machine are the tools she uses to fashion her dreams from the whole cloth of her life's experiences. "…Nottage's play has a delicacy and eloquence that seem absolutely right for the time she is depicting…" –*NY Daily News.* "…thoughtful, affecting…The play offers poignant commentary on an era when the cut and color of one's dress—and of course, skin—determined whom one could and could not marry, sleep with, even talk to in public." –*Variety.* [2M, 4W] ISBN: 0-8222-2009-1

★ **BROOKLYN BOY by Donald Margulies.** A witty and insightful look at what happens to a writer when his novel hits the bestseller list. "The characters are beautifully drawn, the dialogue sparkles…" –*nytheatre.com.* "Few playwrights have the mastery to smartly investigate so much through a laugh-out-loud comedy that combines the vintage subject matter of successful writer-returning-to-ethnic-roots with the familiar mid-life crisis." –*Show Business Weekly.* [4M, 3W] ISBN: 0-8222-2074-1

★ **CROWNS by Regina Taylor.** Hats become a springboard for an exploration of black history and identity in this celebratory musical play. "Taylor pulls off a Hat Trick: She scores thrice, turning CROWNS into an artful amalgamation of oral history, fashion show, and musical theater…" –*TheatreMania.com.* "…wholly theatrical…Ms. Taylor has created a show that seems to arise out of spontaneous combustion, as if a bevy of department-store customers simultaneously decided to stage a revival meeting in the changing room." –*NY Times.* [1M, 6W (2 musicians)] ISBN: 0-8222-1963-8

★ **EXITS AND ENTRANCES by Athol Fugard.** The story of a relationship between a young playwright on the threshold of his career and an aging actor who has reached the end of his. "[Fugard] can say more with a single line than most playwrights convey in an entire script…Paraphrasing the title, it's safe to say this drama, making its memorable entrance into our consciousness, is unlikely to exit as long as a theater exists for exceptional work." –*Variety.* "A thought-provoking, elegant and engrossing new play…" –*Hollywood Reporter.* [2M] ISBN: 0-8222-2041-5

★ **BUG by Tracy Letts.** A thriller featuring a pair of star-crossed lovers in an Oklahoma City motel facing a bug invasion, paranoia, conspiracy theories and twisted psychological motives. "…obscenely exciting…top-flight craftsmanship. Buckle up and brace yourself…" –*NY Times.* "…[a] thoroughly outrageous and thoroughly entertaining play…the possibility of enemies, real and imagined, to squash has never been more theatrical." –*A.P.* [3M, 2W] ISBN: 0-8222-2016-4

★ **THOM PAIN (BASED ON NOTHING) by Will Eno.** An ordinary man muses on childhood, yearning, disappointment and loss, as he draws the audience into his last-ditch plea for empathy and enlightenment. "It's one of those treasured nights in the theater—treasured nights anywhere, for that matter—that can leave you both breathless with exhilaration and…in a puddle of tears." –*NY Times.* "Eno's words…are familiar, but proffered in a way that is constantly contradictory to our expectations. Beckett is certainly among his literary ancestors." –*nytheatre.com.* [1M] ISBN: 0-8222-2076-8

★ **THE LONG CHRISTMAS RIDE HOME by Paula Vogel.** Past, present and future collide on a snowy Christmas Eve for a troubled family of five. "…[a] lovely and hauntingly original family drama…a work that breathes so much life into the theater." –*Time Out.* "…[a] delicate visual feast…" –*NY Times.* "…brutal and lovely…the overall effect is magical." –*NY Newsday.* [3M, 3W] ISBN: 0-8222-2003-2

DRAMATISTS PLAY SERVICE, INC.
440 Park Avenue South, New York, NY 10016 212-683-8960 Fax 212-213-1539
postmaster@dramatists.com   www.dramatists.com